KU-621-302

Wilson ONWINE 2020

THE WINES TO DRINK THIS YEAR

CITY OF DUBLIN
PUBLIC LIBRARIES
WORN-OUT BOOK
WITHDRAWN
TRANSFERRED.

IRISH TIMES BOOKS

in association with

Santa Rita

Published by: The Irish Times Limited
Editor: Joe Breen
Design & Layout: Angelo McGrath (The Irish Times)
Photographer: Breffni Ryan | breffniryan.com | +353 86 252 7506
Printed by: Printrun

© John Wilson 2019
© The Irish Times 2019
© Breffni Ryan (images) 2019

ISBN 9781999307813

All rights reserved. No part of this publication may be
reproduced, stored in a retrieval system, or transmitted in any
form or by any means without the prior written consent of The
Irish Times Limited, or under terms agreed with the appropriate
reprographic rights organisation or as expressly permitted by law.

THE WINES TO DRINK THIS YEAR

Welcome to the sixth edition of Wilson on Wine, a selection of my favourite wines on sale in Ireland in every price category. As someone who has spent almost all my adult life tasting wine for a living - you know the line, it's a tough job but someone has it do it - I still sometimes have to pinch myself because I'm lucky to have tasted so many great, truly exciting wines over the past 12 months.

I am often asked is it difficult to come up with more than 160 new wines each year? It is the opposite. Every year as deadline looms I stare at a shortlist of 200 plus great wines and agonise over which bottles will not make the cut. I still have a list of 50 or so wines 'in waiting'. Overall I include as many wines as possible that are new to the Irish market. Having said that, some wines are listed again because they are just too good to leave out.

This year we have a number of firsts - China, Croatia, Uruguay, Georgia, Wales, yes Wales. Where will it end? With more Irish wine I hope. As our climate changes, and know-how improves, vineyards are being planted in countries that until now were never considered viable for viticulture. Of course, climate change in general poses great threats, both now, and into the future. Viticulture will not be immune, but the range and origins of wines available today is mind-boggling – ten years ago few wine guides would have included bottles from countries such as China and Wales.

Another man-made disaster, Brexit, could also have a huge impact on wine in Ireland. At time of writing it is not clear how it will work out, but given our economic ties to the UK, particularly in the wine trade, a happy ending is unlikely.

As with last year, I include a section on natural wines. I dislike the term, as it implies that all other wines are unnatural. Until there is a legal definition, the lines between natural and conventional wines will always be blurred. That said, I believe that most great wines are made by producers who try to minimise the use of sprays in the vineyard, and who interfere in the winemaking process as little as possible.

Small independent wine shops and off-licences continue to struggle against the might of the larger multiples. I have no quarrel with the supermarkets and discounters they play an important role in the wine business by offering a range of very affordable wines. I tasted a huge number of them for this book, but there are very few that excite, and so, relatively speaking, very few are included. In addition, the plethora of special offers, discounts and multi-buys make it difficult to know where true value lies.

There is a small group of specialist importers and retailers who know and love wine, and go to great lengths to source most of the really exciting wines that appear in this book. It would certainly be a very drab life without them, so please give them your support!

We are rightly concerned about how much alcohol we consume and many of us want to drink wines with a lower abv. However, several studies show that, tasted blind, we generally go for more powerful wines. It seems we like the taste and the rich mouthfeel that higher alcohol levels bring to wine, but don't like the side-effects! Yet there are times, especially during the cold winter nights, when we yearn for something rich, rounded and smooth. The trick is to drink less of these wines, and to drink them with food.

Once again I am grateful to Santa Rita and The Irish Times for their support; without them, this book would not be possible. As always, I would be delighted to hear from you the reader with any comments or suggestions as to how I can improve the book next year.

Happy drinking!
John Wilson

Email wilsononwinw@gmail.com
Blog www.wilsononwine.ie
🐦 @wilsononwine
📘 Wilsononwine

IRISH TIMES BOOKS

in association with

Santa Rita®

NATURAL WINE

Can a wine from a large producer, made without sulphur, produced using organic grapes, be called natural? Many fans of natural wine believe it is all about small artisan producers and any attempt by 'big wine' to muscle in on their territory should be resisted.

There are also many small artisan producers featured in this book who make great 'low intervention' wines but would not consider their wines natural. If such a producer adds a yeast nutrient (the scary sounding diamonnium phosphate) to keep a ferment going or to prevent reduction, or a small amount of sulphur at bottling, is the wine therefore unnatural? Would we prefer to drink a stinky half-fermented wine filled with carbon dioxide?

I have a section that includes some natural wines, but there are many other low-intervention wines elsewhere in the book that could have been included. I believe that the quality of natural wines has improved over the last year, with fewer clearly faulty wines; either that or I have been very lucky. We should all be in favour of wines made from organic grapes with fewer additives and treatments, but not at the expense of a satisfying glass of good wine.

FOOD & WINE

As in previous years, I make recommendations on what to eat with each wine. Some are based on my own 'testing', others the result of my fertile imagination! Sometimes I think we worry a little too much about finding the perfect match for a wine. When friends or family gather around, it is all about enjoying the company. Wine is an important part of the proceedings, but it is not the main event. Having said that, if you take a little care when choosing your wine, it will surely add to the occasion.

Why not take a bottle of your favourite wine and try a glass with a few different foods? Matching food and wine is not a scientific process. It is subjective and you should feel free to drink any wine with any food you like. Trial, and the odd error, are all part of the learning process. We have all been told to match white wines with fish, and red with meat. It does make some sense to match red wine with the stronger flavours of red meat, and the crisp acidity of white wines with seafood. But lighter reds can go very well with salmon or tuna, and meats such as chicken and pork (as well as cheese) are often equally good with white wine.

When choosing a bottle of wine, think about the weight of a dish; food rich in flavour will probably go better with a full-bodied wine. Then take a look at the accompanying sauces, marinades and dips as well. A sauce packed with chili and spices will certainly need something equally flavoursome. Not surprisingly the wines of a particular area often go well with the local foods.

If this all seems a little too complicated, remember that most food tastes better with wine, and wine invariably tastes better with food!

Leabharlanna Poiblí Chathair Baile Átha Cliath
Dublin City Public Libraries

THE WINE STYLES

Describing wines is never easy or exact; one person's cherries can be another's plums. I have tried to keep the tasting notes as short as possible and to avoid very florid descriptions. I hope that they will give you a real sense of the wine's taste. I also give a possible food match with each wine, some fairly specific but most are very broad suggestions. Matching food and wine can be complicated. It is not just about the main constituent of a meal; the sauce, the accompanying vegetables, fruits and herbs all make a difference. I do include quite a few all-purpose wines that can be happily matched with most foods. Instead of simply listing the wines in price order or by country, I think it more useful to divide them up by style; this should make it easier to access the kind of wine you like, and to encourage you to experiment a little. The categories are also colour-coded to aid navigation.

SPARKLING WINES 1-22
Self-explanatory I hope!

CRISP REFRESHING WHITE WINES 23-50
Light, zesty dry white wines with plenty of refreshing acidity. They generally have less alcohol and lighter fruits than those in the Fresh & Fruity category. Good to drink on their own, or with lighter dishes.

FRESH AND FRUITY WHITE WINES 51-92
White wines with plenty of mouth-watering fruits balanced by good acidity. Generally unoaked, with more fruit and flavour than the Crisp Refreshing Whites. Fine to drink on their own or with richer fish and salad dishes.

RICH AND ROUNDED WHITE WINES 93-116
Bigger, more powerful textured white wines, some oak-aged, that fill the mouth with flavour. These wines are best served alongside food.

ROSÉ WINES 117-124
Rosé wines vary in style from crisp and dry to soft and sweet. This year we include three wines, all firmly in the former camp.

LIGHT AND ELEGANT RED WINES 125-194

Restrained, lighter wines with more subtle fruits. They are lower in alcohol and have light tannins. These can be drunk on their own or with lighter foods.

ROUNDED AND FRUITY RED WINES 195-238

These red wines have plenty of smooth rounded fruits and moderate tannins; good with many foods.

RICH AND FULL-BODIED RED WINES 239-276

The biggest and most powerful red wines, robust and rich in alcohol and flavour. Some have high levels of tannin too. These wines are best drunk alongside substantial dishes.

NATURAL WINES 277-296

There is no legal definition for the term natural wine. However, it is generally accepted to refer to wines that are made using organic or biodynamic grapes, with as little intervention as possible, including additives and other treatments.

FINE WINES 297-330

These are wines whose complexity, depth and sheer quality sets them apart. They usually are expensive, but not necessarily so. Most, but not all, have the ability to improve with age.

FORTIFIED WINES 331-348

Wines such as sherry, port and madeira receive a fortifying boost of brandy to increase their alcohol in the winemaking process. A great many are dry, others are sweet, but don't ignore them - these are amongst the most complex wines of all, and some go really well with food too.

INDEX BY STYLE COUNTRY PRICE

*Price when on promotion

Wine	Country	Price	Page no.
Friulano 2018, Volpe Pasini, Friuli Colli Orientale	Italy	€15.50	62
Gambellara Classico 2018, Cantina di Gambellara	Italy	€15.95	64
Cucú 2018, Barco del Corneta, Rueda	Spain	€17.75	66
Amalaya Torrontés Riesling 2018, Calchaquí Valley	Argentina	€17.99	68
Herdade de Grous Branco 2017, VR Alentejo	Portugal	€18	70
Terroir Unico Chardonnay 2018, Vina Zorzal	Argentina	€18.50	72
Albariño 2017, Rías Baixas, Lagar de Costa	Spain	€19.95/ 16.95*	74
Clima 2016, Vale da Capucha IG Lisboa	Portugal	€20	76
Reto 2018, Manchuela, Bodegas Ponce	Spain	€21	78
Terlaner Cuvée 2018, Trentino	Italy	€24.75	80
Leirana, Albariño, Forjas del Salnes 2018, Rías Baixas	Spain	€25	82
Giacomo Fenocchio Roero Arneis 2017	Italy	€26	84
Adèle 2018, Eric Texier,	France	€26	86
Piedradolce Etna Bianco 2018	Italy	€27	88
69 Arrobas 2017, Rías Baixas, Bodegas Albamar	Spain	€34	90
St. Joseph 'Grand Duc du Montillet' 2017, Domaine du Monteillet	France	€38	92

Rich & Rounded White Wines

Wine	Country	Price	Page no.
Réserve de Boulas Laudun Côtes du Rhône Villages 2018	France	€13.30	96
d'Arenberg Hermit Crab 2016, Mclaren Vale	Australia	€16.95	98
Old Vine Reserve Chenin Blanc 2018, Ken Forrester Vineyards, Stellenbosch	South Africa	€17.95	100
Quinta de Saes Tobias Encruzado, Dão 2018	Portgual	€18.95	102
Viré-Clessé 2017, Les Pierres Blanches, Domaine André Bonhomme	France	€22.95	104
Zephyr 2017, Les Deux Cols, Côtes du Rhône	France	€22.95	106
Terrasse 2017, Keermont, Stellenbosch	South Africa	€30	108
Kumeu River Estate Chardonnay 2018, Auckland	N Zealand	€33.00	110
Arbois 'Cuvée d'Automne' Domaine de la Pinte 2016	France	€33.50	112
Clos Saint Yves 2016 Savannières, Domaine des Baumard	France	€36.75	114
Kershaw Clonal Selection Chardonnay 2017	South Africa	€54	116

*Price when on promotion

Wine	Country	Price	Page no.
Rosé Wines			
Domaine Bastide Neuve 2018, Rosé d'Oc	France	**€10.50**	120
Réserve du Boulas Côtes du Rhône Rosé 2018	France	**€13.30**	122
Ahearne Rosine Hvar 2017	Croatia	**€38.99**	124
Light and Elegant Red Wines			
Château Roc de Villepreux 2016, Bordeaux			
Supérieur	France	**€10.50**	128
Wildflower Pinot Noir 2018	Romania	**€13.95/€8.35***	130
Pinot Noir, Domaine de la Renne, Val de Loire	France	**€14.15**	132
Mitchell & Son Claret 2015, Bordeaux			
Superieur	France	**€15**	134
Rosso Piceno 2017, Saladini Pilastri	Italy		
Beaujolais '69' 2017, Christophe Coquard	France	**€15.95**	136
Marzemino 2018 Roberta Fugatti, IGT		**€16**	138
Marzemino della Vallagarina	Italy	**€16**	140
Colle Morino 2017, Barba, Montepulciano			
d'Abruzzo	Italy	**€16.50**	142
Le Vin est une Fête 2017, Côtes du			
Marmandais, Elian da Ros	France	**€16.95**	144
La Roncière Pinot Noir 2017, Val de Loire,			
André Vatan	France	**€17.00**	146
Quinta de Saes Tobias Tinto, Dão 2016	Portugal		
Tolloy Blauburgunder / Pino Nero 2017 Sud		**€18.95**	148
Tirol-Alto Adige	Italy	**€18.95**	150
Fleurie Tradition 2016, Domaine de la Madone	France		
di Gino 2017, Rosso Piceno San Lorenzo	Italy	**€20.95**	152
Pinot Noir Les Petits Apôtres 2018, Domaine		**€21.50**	154
de Bon Augures	France	**€22**	156
Domaine Lardy Moulin-à-Vent Vieilles Vignes			
2016	France	**€22**	158
Volcánico País 2018, A los Viñateros Bravos,			
Itata	Chile	**€23.85**	160
Bourgueil 2017 La Coudraye, Y. Amirault	France		
Masetto Nero 2016, Endrizzi, Vigneti delle		**€24**	162
Dolomiti	Italy	**€24.95**	164
Freisa d'Asti Secco 2015, Tenuta Olim Bauda	Italy		
Drink Me Nat 'Cool' 2017, 1 litre bottle,		**€24.95**	166
Bairrada, Niepoort	Portugal	**€25**	168
Camiño Real 2017 Ribera Sacra, Guímaro	Spain		
Ch. Jean Faux Les Sources 2014, Bordeaux		**€26**	170
Supérieur	France	**€26**	172
Folk Machine 'Parts & Labor' Red 2016,			
California	USA	**€26**	174

*Price when on promotion

Wine	Country	Price	Page no.
Silice 2017, Ribeira Sacra	Spain	€26.95	176
Domaine Desvignes Morgon 'La Voûte St-Vincent' 2017	France	€27	178
Framingham Pinot Noir 2016, Marlborough	NZealand	€27.99	180
Chinon Vieilles Vignes 2017, Domaine Philippe Alliet	France	€29.50	182
Le Temps des C(e)rises 2014, Santenay, Domaine Olivier	France	€29.95/23.95*	184
Lomba des Ares 2016, Ribeira Sacra, Fedellos do Couto	Spain	€31	186
Sancerre Rouge La Croix du Roy 2014, Lucien Crochet	France	€34	188
Bourgogne Pinot Noir 2015, Sylvain Pataille	France	€35	190
Rouge-Gorge 2017, Coteaux du Loir Domaine de Bellivière	France	€39	192
La Porte Saint Jean, Saumur 2015 , Sylvain Dittière	France	€39.50	194
Rounded and Fruity Red Wines			
Aldi Exquisite Collection Pinot Noir, Wairarapa	N Zealand	€9.99	198
Santa Rita 120 Cabernet Franc	Chile	€12.50	200
Ciello Rosso 2018 IGP Terre Siciliane	Italy	€12.95	202
Les Vignes d'Oc Rouge Grenache / Merlot 2018, Languedoc	France	€12.99	204
T'Air Syrah, Pays d'Oc 2017	France	€14.50	206
Rosso Piceno DOC, Cantina dei Colli Ripani 2018	Italy	€14.95	208
Ars in Vitro 0216, Tandem, Valle de Yerri, Navarra	Spain	€14.95	210
Ch. Bellevue-La-Forêt 2016, Fronton	France	€16.00	212
Altos Las Hormigas Tinto 2017, Mendoza	Argentina	€17.99	214
Viano 'Hillside" Red NV	USA	€18	216
Clos des Fous 'Pour ma Gueule" 2017, Itata Valley	Chile	€19.99	218
Sherazadze Donnafugatta 2018, Sicilia DOC, Nero d'Avola	Italy	€23	220
Montes Outer Limits "Old Roots" Cinsault 2018, Itata	Chile	€23.99	222
Cuvée Equinox 2017, Crozes-Hermitage, Domaine des Lises	France	€24	224
Bourgogne 2017, Domaine Derey Frères	France	€24.50	226
Johanneshöhe Blaufränkisch 2017, Burgenland, Prieler	Austria	€25	228
Eggo Tinto de Tiza Malbec 2016, Viña Zorzal	Argentina	€25	230
Daniel Bouland Morgon Courcelette Vieilles Vignes 2016	France	€26	232
Imaginador 2017, Pedro Parra, Itata	Chile	€26.99	234

*Price when on promotion

Wine	Country	Price	Page no.
Chemin des Fonts 2018, Les Deux Cols, Côtes du Rhône	France	€28.50	236
Iroulégy Tradition 2015, Domaine Arretxea	France	€29.50	238
Rich and Full-bodied Red Wines			
Merinas Old Vine Tempranillo 2018, Bodegas Fontana, Uclés	Spain	€10.50	242
Canfo Tempranillo 2017, Castilla-La Mancha, Bodegas Campos Reales	Spain	€13	244
Passo Sardo 2016, Cannonau di Sardegna	Italy	€14.00	246
Petit Saó 2015, Costers del Segre	Spain	€15.95	248
Côtes du Rhône Saint-Esprit 2017, Delas	France	€16.95	250
Jarrarte 2018 Rioja Joven, Abel Mendoza	Spain	€17	252
Carmen Gran Reserva Cabernet Sauvignon 2017 SV Maipo	Chile	€18.50	254
Ruminat Primitivo 2018, IGT Terre di Chieti	Italy	€18.95	256
D.O.C. Malbec 2016, Norton, Luján de Cuyo, Mendoza	Argentina	18.95/12.95*	258
Dedicace 2017, Lirac, Domaine Coudoulis	France	19.95/26.95*	260
Mimetic 2018, Gallinas de Piel, Calatayud	Spain	€19.99	262
Garzón Tannat Reserva 2017,	Uruguay	€20	264
Chateau Beauchene Premier Terroir 2016, Côtes du Rhône	France	€20	266
Langhe Nebbiolo 2016, Pian delle Mole, Giula Negri	Italy	€27	268
Rioja Reserva 2012, La Granja Nuestra Senora de Remelluri, Remelluri	Spain	€32	270
Selección de Bodega Malbec 2016, Dona Paula, Alluvia Vineyard, Gualtallary	Argentina	€35	272
Gianni Brunelli Rosso di Montalcino 2017	Italy	€38	274
Anthill Farms 2016 Syrah, Campbell Ranch Vineyard, Sonoma Coast	USA	€40	276
Natural Wines			
Custoza Boscroi 2018, Monte dei Roari	Italy	€17	280
Bardolino "Reboi" 2018, Monte dei Roari	Italy	€17	282
Ink 2018, Judith Beck, Burgenland	Austria	€17.95	284
Vola Vole 2018, Trebbiano d'Abruzzo	Italy	€17.95/13.95*	286
Pheasant's Tears Saperavi 2018	Georgia	€23.95	288
Rivera del Notro 2017, Itata, Roberto Henriques	Chile		
Verdicchio dei Castelli di Jeso Classico Superiore		€24	290
Capovolto 2018, La Marca di San Michele	Italy	€24.00	292
Unlitro 2018, Ampelia IGT Costa Toscana	Italy		
Benje Tinto, Envínate, Ycoden-Daute-Isora,		€24.50	294
Tenerife 2017	Spain	€28.00	296

*Price when on promotion

Wine	Country	Price	Page no.
Fine Wines			
Sandhi Pinot Noir 2016, Sta. Rita Hills, California	USA	**€38**	300
Chablis 1er cru Vauleront 2015,La Chablisienne	France	**€40**	302
Bodega Colomé 'Auténtico' Salta Malbec 2017	Argentina	**€41.99**	304
Etna Rosso Guardioloa 2016, Tenuta delle Terre Nere	Italy	**€45**	306
Viña Tondonia 2005, Bodegas López de Heredia, Rioja Reserva Blanco	Spain	**€45**	308
Pavillon de Léoville Poyferré 2015, St. Julien	France	**€45**	310
As Sortes 2017, Rafael Palacios, Valdeorras	Spain	**€46**	312
Brunello di Montalcino 2014, Col d'Orcia	Italy	**€48**	314
2016 Chablis 1er Cru Mont de Milieu, Domaine Christophe	France	**€49**	316
Pretty Pony 2013, Kanaan Winery, Ningxia Helan Mountain	China	**€49.99**	318
Sandhi Sanford & Benedict Chardonnay 2016	USA	**€50**	320
Two Paddocks 'The Fusilier' Pinot Noir 2018, Central Otago	N Zealand	**€50**	322
Trefiano 2015, Carmignano Riserva 2015, Capezzana	Italy	**€54.99**	324
Barolo Castiglione 2015, Vietti, Piemonte	Italy	**€55**	326
Tolpuddle Vineyard Pinot Noir 2015, Coal River, Tasmania	Australia	**€62.99**	328
Corison Cabernet Sauvignon 2014, Napa Valley, California	USA	**€132**	330
Fortified Wines			
Marks & Spencer Manzanilla	Spain	**€12**	334
Gabriela Pago Balbaina, Sanchez Ayala, Manzanilla	Spain	**€12.30***	336
Callejuela Manzanilla Fina NV	Spain	**€18**	338
Oloroso, Marqués de Poley , Montilla-Moriles, Toro Albalá	Spain	**€19.95**	340
Taylor's Late-Bottled Vintage Port 2014	Portugal	**€24**	342
El Maestro Sierra Fino	Spain	**€25.99**	344
Ten Year Old Malvasia, Barbeito, Madeira, NV	Portgual	**€39.99**	346
Taylor's Finest Vintage Port 2017		**€120**	348

*per 1/2 bottle

SPARKLING WINES

1

M&S Cava Brut NV
Spain 11.5% **€10.50** Vegan

3

STOCKISTS: Marks & Spencer, Marksandspencer.com/ie

M&S Cava Brut NV

TASTING NOTE
A very friendly easy-drinking sparkling wine with fresh ripe pear and apple fruits.

DRINK WITH
Parties, an aperitif, or any mini-celebration.

STYLE
Sparkling

GRAPE VARIETY
60% Xarel·lo, 30% Macabeo, 10% Parellada

BACKSTORY
Is Cava the new Prosecco? Certainly this fruit-filled fizz offers a viable alternative at a very competitive price.

2

**Aldi Exquisite Crémant
d'Alsace 2017**
France 12.5% **€12.99**

5

CRÉMANT D'ALSACE

Brut Prestige

STOCKISTS: Aldi, Aldi.ie

Aldi Exquisite Crémant d'Alsace 2017

TASTING NOTE
Light and refreshing with clean pear and apple fruits, and a nicely rounded finish.

DRINK WITH
This would get your party off to a great start, or as an aperitif before dinner.

STYLE
Sparkling

GRAPE VARIETY
63% Auxerrois, 25% Pinot Gris, 8% Pinot Blanc, 4% Riesling

BACKSTORY
Every edition of WoW has featured the excellent Aldi Crémant de Jura, which, for years, has been the best value sparkling wine available here. Sadly this has been discontinued. In its place, the Exquisite Crémant d'Alsace, made from a blend of grapes, is certainly a worthy successor.

3 **Jansz Tasmania Premium Cuvée NV**
Australia 12% **€35**

STOCKISTS: Baggot Street Wines, Dublin 4,
baggotstreetwines.com; O'Briens, obrienswine.ie.

Jansz Tasmania Premium Cuvée NV

TASTING NOTE
Moreish ripe fruit gives this sparkling wine a tantalising richness with subtle brioche and toasted hazelnuts lingering nicely on the palate. Very stylish.

DRINK WITH
An elegant and unusual aperitif; or pair with oysters, lighter Chinese seafood or chicken dishes.

STYLE
Sparkling

GRAPE VARIETY
55% Chardonnay, 45% Pinot Noir

BACKSTORY
Australian winemakers have long known that much of their finest Chardonnay and Pinot Noir comes from the cool-climate island of Tasmania. Here both varieties are used to create an excellent sparkling wine. Elsewhere in the book there is a still Pinot Noir from Tasmania.

4 Bollinger Special Cuvée Champagne NV
France 12% €55.65

9

STOCKISTS: O'Briens, obrienswine.ie; Donnybrook Fair, donnybrookfair.ie; Bradleys Off-licence, Cork, bradleysofflicence. ie; Clontarf Wines, Dublin 3 clontarfwines. ie; The Corkscrew, Dublin 2, thecorkscrew.ie; Ely 64, Glasthule, Ely64. com; Mitchell & Son, Dublin 1, Sandycove, and Avoca, Kilmacanogue & Dunboyne, mitchellandson.com; Wines on the Green, Dublin 2, celticwhiskeyshop.com; wineonline.ie

Bollinger Special Cuvée Champagne NV

TASTING NOTE
Bollinger is a wonderfully distinctive Champagne, full in body with rich, complex flavours of brioche, toasted almonds and ripe pear fruits.

DRINK WITH
A Champagne that really deserves to be drunk alongside food; scallops, lobster or poached chicken would all do nicely.

STYLE
Sparkling

GRAPE VARIETY
Chardonnay, Pinot Noir, Pinot Meunier

BACKSTORY
One of the great names in Champagne, Bollinger continues to produce high quality wines with real flair and personality.

5

Ruinart R de Ruinart Champagne NV
France 12% €58.40

STOCKISTS: Jus de Vine, Portmarnock, jusdevine.ie; McCambridges, Galway, Mccambridges.com; Mitchell & Son, Dublin 1, Sandycove, and Avoca, Kilmacanogue & Dunboyne, mitchellandson.com; Grapevine, Dalkey, onthegrapevine.ie; Ely 64, Glasthule, Ely64.com; The Corkscrew, Dublin 2, thecorkscrew.ie; Wines on the Green, Dublin 2, Celticwhiskeyshop.com; O'Briens, obrienswine.ie; Worldwide Wines, Waterford, worldwidewines.ie; Bradleys Off-licence, Cork, bradleysofflicence.ie; O'Donovan's, Cork, Odonovansofflicence.com.

Ruinart R de Ruinart Champagne NV

TASTING NOTE
Medium-bodied with elegant peach and dried fruits, enhanced by refreshing notes of citrus peel. A complex, very attractive Champagne.

DRINK WITH
Great on its own, but the richness would work perfectly with scallops.

STYLE
Sparkling

GRAPE VARIETY
Chardonnay, Pinot Noir, Pinot Meunier

BACKSTORY
Founded in 1729, Ruinart is one of the oldest Champagne houses. It has a unique chalk cellar dating back to Roman times. The company is best known for its Blanc de Blancs, but all of the wines, including the 'R', are well worth seeking out.

6

Champagne Delamotte Blanc de Blancs NV, Le Mesnil-sur-Oger
France 12% €60

STOCKISTS:
Grapevine, Dalkey, onthegrapevine.ie; Mitchell & Son, Dublin 1, Sandycove, and Avoca, Kilmacanogue & Dunboyne, mitchellandson.com; Deveney's, D14.

Champagne Delamotte Blanc de Blancs NV, Le Mesnil-sur-Oger

TASTING NOTE
Ultra-refined, fresh, crisp, Champagne with elegant, concentrated, yeasty, toasted notes that come from aged Chardonnay. Bone dry, lean and magnificent.

DRINK WITH
A plate of very fresh oysters would be perfect.

STYLE
Sparkling

GRAPE VARIETY
Chardonnay

BACKSTORY
Champagne Delamotte is under the same ownership as Salon, one of the greatest producers in Champagne; run by the same team, both specialise in Blanc de Blancs, or wines made from Chardonnay. Only released when mature, the wines have a wonderful austere purity.

7

Champagne Louis Roederer Brut Premier NV
France 12% €62

STOCKISTS: Joyce's Supermarket, Joycesupermarket.ie: Jus de Vine, Portmarnock, jusdevine. ie; Dollard & Co., Dublin 2, Dollardandco.ie; Grapevine, Dalkey, onthegrapevine.ie; O'Briens, obrienswine.ie.

Champagne Louis Roederer Brut Premier NV

TASTING NOTE
Ripe peaches, subtle brioche and toasted nuts with
a lively perfectly integrated acidity. A seductive, rich,
creamy Champagne.

DRINK WITH
Good Champagne goes well with a wide range of
foods, with fish and chicken being the standout options.

STYLE
Sparkling

GRAPE VARIETY
Chardonnay, Pinot Noir, Pinot Meunier

BACKSTORY
This wine also featured last year; alongside Bollinger
and Charles Heidsieck, it remains one of my favourite
Champagnes. The family-owned firm of Louis Roederer
is in the process of converting its entire 230 hectare
domaine to biodynamic viticulture.

8 Charles Heidsieck Brut Réserve Champagne NV
France 12% **€70** Vegan

STOCKISTS: Alain & Christine's, Kenmare, acwine.ie; Baggot Street Wines, Baggot St., baggotstreetwines.com; Blackrock Cellar, Co Dublin, blackrockcellar.com; Clontarf Wines, Dublin 3, clontarfwines.ie; Donnybrook Fair, donnybrookfair.ie; Ely Wine Store - Maynooth, Ely 64 Wine,Co Dublin 64wine.ie; Fallon & Byrne, Dublin 2, fallonandbyrne.com; Green Man Wines, Terenure, greenmanwines.ie; Jus de Vine, Portmarnock, Co Dublin, jusdevine.ie; La Touche Wines, latouchewines4u.ie; Martin's Off-Licence, Dublin 3, martinsofflicence.ie; Mitchell & Son, Dublin 1, Sandycove, and Avoca, Kilmacanogue & Dunboyne, mitchellandson.com; , Redmonds of Ranelagh, redmonds.ie; O'Briens, obriens.ie; Stationtostation.ie; Thomas's of Foxrock; The Vintry, Dublin 6 vintry.ie; Whelehans Wines, Co Dublin, whelehanswines.ie; World Wide Wines, worldwidewines.ie; wineonline.ie.

17

Charles Heidsieck Brut Réserve Champagne NV

TASTING NOTE
Subtle and elegant, with succulent peaches and pears,
overlaid with toasted nuts and brioche.

DRINK WITH
Champagne goes well with many foods, including fish
& chips, but this with a buttery lobster dish would be
heavenly.

STYLE
Sparkling

GRAPE VARIETY
65% Pinot Meunier, 20% Pinot Noir, 15%

BACKSTORY
Charles Heidsieck was the original 'Champagne Charlie',
the man responsible for making Champagne the most
popular celebration drink in the U.S.A. He was arrested
as a spy during the civil war, causing an international
incident, but was later freed.

9

**Ancre Hill Blanc de Noir
N.V., Monmouth, Wales**
Wales 10% **€70** Biodynamic

19

STOCKISTS:
Green Man Wines,
Dublin 6, greenmanwines.ie; Alex Findlater, Limerick;
alexfindlaterandco.ie

Ancre Hill Blanc de Noir N.V., Monmouth, Wales

TASTING NOTE
Lean and angular with precise ripe red fruits - strawberries and raspberries; austere and bone dry, showing a lovely maturity – biscuits and brioche. Great finesse and a fine finish.

DRINK WITH
Grilled fish, shellfish, raw or cooked. Half a dozen oysters?

STYLE
Sparkling

GRAPE VARIETY
Pinot Noir

BACKSTORY
Yes, Wales! A biodynamic estate making really interesting grown-up bone-dry fizz. This is 100% Pinot Noir, a blend of 2013 and 2014, and is aged on the lees for at least two years.

10

Krug Grandé Cuvée Brut N.V., Champagne
France 12% €215

STOCKISTS: Jus de Vine, Portmarnock, jusdevine.ie; O'Briens, obrienswine.ie; Grapevine, Dalkey, onthegrapevine.ie; Gibney's, Malahide, gibneys.com; Mitchell & Son, Dublin 1, Sandycove, and Avoca, Kilmacanogue & Dunboyne, mitchellandson.com.

Krug Grandé Cuvée Brut N.V., Champagne

TASTING NOTE
A rich, powerful, complex wine that seduces with every sip; waves of toasted hazelnuts, apples, pears, dried fruits and lemon peel; rich yet refreshing, this is the ultimate Champagne.

DRINK WITH
Great on its own, but even better with turbot, black sole, oysters, prawns or scallops.

STYLE
Sparkling

GRAPE VARIETY
Chardonnay, Pinot Noir, Pinot Meunier

BACKSTORY
Can a wine be worth €200? Krug is a legendary Champagne house, producing small quantities of exquisite wines. Each year, they release a new numbered edition of the multi-vintage Grande Cuvçe, created from scratch. As with luxury items such as Hermés bags or Ferrari cars, each of us must decide if we think it worth the price.

CRISP
REFRESHING
WHITE WINES

11 Solto Escola 2016, Vinho Verde
Portugal 12% **€13.95**

STOCKISTS: Searsons, Monkstown, searsons.com;
D-Six Wines, Dublin 6; peggykellys.ie.

Solto Escola 2016, Vinho Verde

TASTING NOTE
Refreshing with vibrant citrus and peach fruits. Despite the lightness, it has good concentration and length. Great value for money too.

DRINK WITH
We drank this with queen scallops simply seared with butter and lemon juice.

STYLE
Crisp refreshing white wines

GRAPE VARIETY
Arinto, Avesso, Loureiro, Trajadura

BACKSTORY
Vinho Verde has come on in leaps and bounds; these days there are fewer semi-sweet, green, herbaceous wines and more light, succulent and concentrated versions that are perfect with shellfish. Anselmo Mendes seems to have a hand in just about everything that is going on in this part of Portugal. Not only does he have his own winery (available through Wines on the Green) but he advises a number of other producers too, including this one.

12 Muros Antigos Escolha Vinho Verde 2018
Portugal 12.5% **€14**

STOCKISTS: Wines on The Green, celticwhiskeyshop.com

Muros Antigos EscholaVinho Verde 2018

TASTING NOTE
Floral aromas, succulent green apples and pears, with
zesty citrus peel. Fresh as a spring morning. Amazing
value for money!

DRINK WITH
With leafy light salads featuring soft goat's cheese, herbs
and lemon.

STYLE
Crisp Refreshing White Wines

GRAPE VARIETY
40% Loureiro, 40% Avesso, 20% Alvarinho

BACKSTORY
Wines on the Green has four excellent wines, all from
winemaker Anselmo Mendes, who is an influential figure
in this part of the world - the Muros Antigos Alvarinho
(€18.50), the Contacto (€20) and the Muros de Melgaço
(€27.50). All are well worth trying.

13 Tahbilk Marsanne 2018, Nagambie Lakes, Central Victoria Australia 12% €14.25

STOCKISTS: Wines Direct, Mullingar, and Arnotts, Dublin, winesdirect.ie

Tahbilk Marsanne 2018, Nagambie Lakes, Central Victoria

TASTING NOTE
A wonderful wine and a steal at this price. Zesty lemon, apples, and stone fruits with a touch of honey. Drink now or keep for 10 years plus.

DRINK WITH
With a spicy pork and pepper stir fry.

STYLE
Crisp Refreshing White Wines

GRAPE VARIETY
Marsanne

BACKSTORY
This is one of my favourite wines, and one that remains one of the great wine bargains; drink it young for its exuberant lime and peach fruits, or a few years later when it takes on a glorious waxy nutty character. Either way it is a steal.

14

Arinto 2018, Vinho Verde, Quinta, Picouto de Cima
Portugal 12% **€14.95**

STOCKISTS: O'Briens, obrienswine.ie

Arinto 2018, Vinho Verde, Quinta Picouto de Cima

TASTING NOTE
Racy green apple fruits, with a light sparkle; slakes the thirst and gets the mouth watering.

DRINK WITH
As an aperitif with nibbles, raw seafood, sushi or oily fish such as mackerel.

STYLE
Crisp Refreshing White Wines

GRAPE VARIETY
Ugni blanc 45%, Colombard 35%, Sauvignon 10%, Gros Manseng 10%

BACKSTORY
WoW 2020 features a number of great thirst-quenching dry white wines from Portugal, including several from the Vinho Verde region which is now very much back in vogue.

15

Ch. du Coing de St. Fiacre 2017, Muscadet de Sèvre & Maine Sur Lie
France 12% **€16.55**
Lutte Raisonnée

STOCKISTS: Bradleys Off-licence, Cork, bradleysofflicence.ie; Fallon & Byrne, Exchequer St., fallonandbyrne.com; The Corkscrew, Chatham St., thecorkscrew.ie; Le Caveau, Kilkenny, lecaveau.ie; Green Man Wines, Terenure, greenmanwines.ie; Listons, Camden St., listonsfoodstore.ie; MacGuinness Wines, Dundalk, dundalkwines.com; Worldwide Wines, Waterford, worldwidewines.ie

Ch. du Coing de St. Fiacre 2017, Muscadet de Sèvre & Maine Sur Lie

TASTING NOTE
Lively ripe apple and pear fruits, subtle lemon zest and a fine mineral acidity.

DRINK WITH
By itself, with shellfish, or summery salads.

STYLE
Crisp Refreshing White Wines

GRAPE VARIETY
Melon de Bourgogne

BACKSTORY
One of two Muscadets in the book; if you are tiring of Pinot Grigio or Sauvignon Blanc, these wines are well worth trying out.

16

Les Secrets de Sophie Touraine Sauvignon Blanc 2018 Italy 12.5%
€16.95/€12.95*

STOCKISTS: O'Briens, obrienswine.ie

*Price when on promotion

Les Secrets de Sophie Touraine Sauvignon Blanc 2018

TASTING NOTE
Light and spritely with clean and crisp green apple fruits and a snappy dry finish.

DRINK WITH
Goat's cheese salad, tomato salad or greek salad; Sauvignon loves salads!

STYLE
Crisp Refreshing White Wines

GRAPE VARIETY
Sauvignon Blanc

BACKSTORY
A new addition from the Bougrier family who supply O'Briens with a range of great value wines from the Loire Valley.

17 Muscadet de Sèvre & Maine Sur Lie, La Louvetrie 2018
France 12.5% **€17.15** Organic

STOCKISTS: Wines Direct, Mullingar, and Arnott's, Dublin 1, winesdirect.ie

Muscadet de Sèvre & Maine Sur Lie, La Louvetrie 2018

TASTING NOTE
Vibrant, fresh, succulent pear fruits, with a mineral streak. A generous and beautifully balanced Muscadet.

DRINK WITH
Muscadet is perfect with all kinds of shellfish, my favourite match being with fresh oysters.

STYLE
Crisp Refreshing White Wines

GRAPE VARIETY
Melon de Bourgogne

BACKSTORY
I am a huge fan of Muscadet; it is the perfect al fresco summer wine, but can be enjoyed throughout the year either as an aperitif, or with any kind of shellfish.

18
La Raspa Blanco Seco 2017, Bodegas Viñedos Verticales, Sierras de Málaga
Spain 13% €19

STOCKISTS: 64 Wine, Glasthule, 64wine.ie; Matson's, Grange, Bandon; Liston's, Camden St., listonsfoodstore. ie; Baggot Street Wines, Baggot St., baggotstreetwines.com.

La Raspa Blanco Seco 2017, Bodegas Viñedos Verticales, Sierras de Málaga

TASTING NOTE
Fragrant and elegant with floral aromas and delicate but persistent pure tropical fruits. A delight to drink.

DRINK WITH
On its own, or even better, with a plate of prawns to nibble.

STYLE
Crisp Refreshing White Wines

GRAPE VARIETY
Moscatel de Alejandria, Doradilla

BACKSTORY
Viñedos Verticales is a project conjured up in 2015 by two experienced winemakers and friends, Juan Muñoz and Vicente Inat. In a small village in Málaga they work with old local grapes grown on steep slopes, mainly Moscatel, to produce a series of fascinating expressive low-intervention wines.

19 Roka Furmint 2018, Kog, Štajerska
Slovenia 13% **€19.50** Vegan

STOCKISTS: Cabot and Co., Westport, Cabotandco.com; Grapevine, Dalkey, onthegrapevine.ie; PoppySeed, Clarinbridge, PoppySeed.ie; Butler & Byrne, Cong.

Roka Furmint 2018, Kog, Štajerska

TASTING NOTE
Medium-bodied with succulent stone fruits, a touch of ginger spice, and a wonderful lingering finish. This has real depth and interest.

DRINK WITH
Pan-fried white fish - hake or cod, or a plain roast chicken.

STYLE
Crisp Refreshing Whites

GRAPE VARIETY
Furmint

BACKSTORY
The wines made by the Irish husband and wife team of Sinéad and Liam Cabot get better with each vintage. This year the Blaufränkisch will be bottled too late for inclusion, but this award-winning Furmint is worth seeking out. It is certainly the best vintage yet and a seriously good wine.

20 **The Flower and the Bee, Ribeiro, Coto de Gomariz 2018**
Spain 13.5% **€19.95**
Biodynamic not certified.
Vegan friendly.

STOCKISTS:
Green Man Wines, Dublin 6, greenmanwines.ie; Clontarf Wines, Dublin 3 clontarfwines.ie; La Touche, Greystones, Latouchewines4u.ie; Kellys, Dublin 3, kellysofflicence.ie; Crafted, Bennettsbridge Kilkenny; Deveney's D14; Ely 64, Glasthule, Ely64.com; Ardkeen Quality Foodstore, Waterford, Ardkeen.com.

The Flower and the Bee, Ribeiro, Coto de Gomariz 2018

TASTING NOTE
Vibrant, mouth-watering, fresh pear and stone fruits; one of those wines that grows on you with every sip.

DRINK WITH
Richer seafood should do nicely; scallops with pea puree to bring the ripeness out, or a classic prawn cocktail.

STYLE
Crisp Refreshing White Wines

GRAPE VARIETY
Treixadura

BACKSTORY
The Ribeiro is possibly the least well-known of the wine regions of Galicia; however, both red and white wines can be spectacularly good.

21 **Soalheiro Alvarinho 2018, Monçao & Melgaço, Vinho Verde**
Portugal 12.5% **€21** Vegan

STOCKISTS: JNwine.com;
Ely 64, Glasthule, Ely64.com;
The Corkscrew, Dublin 2,
thecorkscrew.ie; Sweeney's D3,
sweeneysd3.ie, The Counter, Letterkenny.

Soalheiro Alvarinho 2018, Monçao & Melgaço, Vinho Verde

TASTING NOTE
A very seductive blend of lemon zest and light tropical fruits – pineapples and mango - with a crisp dry finish. Light and nervy.

DRINK WITH
With mixed seafood or mezze.

STYLE
Crisp Refreshing White Wines

GRAPE VARIETY
Alvarinho

BACKSTORY
One of four Vinho Verdes in the book, proof that this region is producing some really great wines at the moment.

22 Immich-Baterieberg Riesling Detonation 2017, Mosel
Germany 11.5% **€26** Organic

STOCKISTS: Baggot Street Wines, Dublin 4, baggotstreetwines. com; 64wine: Green Man Wines, Dublin 6, greenmanwines.ie; Loose Canon, Dublin 2, loosecanon.ie; Lilliput Stores, Dublin 7, lilliputstores.com.

Immich-Baterieberg Riesling Detonation 2017, Mosel

TASTING NOTE
I love everything about this wine; the pristine fresh peach and zingy lemon zest fruits, the wonderful cleansing mineral acidity, the whiff of smoke, and the excellent length.

DRINK WITH
With fresh crab salads, sashimi, or simply cooked scallops or Dublin Bay prawns.

STYLE
Crisp Refreshing White Wines

GRAPE VARIETY
Riesling

BACKSTORY
One of the most renowned winemakers in Germany, Gernot Kollmann made his name at several other high-quality estates before joining the historic Mosel estate of Immich-Batterieberg in 2009. The four vineyards include unique ancient ungrafted pre-phylloxera vines. The wines are an incredible mix of stunning complex succulent fruit, and mouth-watering refreshing acidity.

23 Trenzado 2018, Bodegas Suerte del Marqués, Tenerife
Spain 12.5% **€26**

STOCKISTS: Ely 64, Glasthule, Ely64.com; Green Man Wines, Dublin 6, greenmanwines.ie; SIYPS.com; Loose Canon, Dublin 2, loosecanon.ie

Trenzado 2018, Bodegas Suerte del Marqués, Tenerife

TASTING NOTE
Clean, appetising and fresh with toasted hazelnuts and textured luscious pears bound up in lemon zest.

DRINK WITH
Perfect on its own or with a plate of cold shellfish.

STYLE
Crisp Refreshing White Wines

GRAPE VARIETY
Listán Blanco, Torrontés

BACKSTORY
There have been vineyards on the Canary Islands for centuries, many of them planted with unique old varieties. It is only in the last few years that young winemakers have rediscovered this lost heritage and begun making exciting wines.

FRESH AND FRUITY
WHITE WINES

24 Tesco Finest Côtes de Gascogne 2018
France   11% **€9**

53

STOCKISTS: Tesco, tesco.ie

Tesco Finest Côtes de Gascogne 2018

TASTING NOTE
Lightly aromatic with clean fresh apple and pear fruits,
with plenty of brisk citrus.

DRINK WITH
On its own, with seafood or fresh goat's cheese salads.

STYLE
Fresh & Fruity White Wines

GRAPE VARIETY
Colombard, Gros Manseng

BACKSTORY
This one should please lovers of Sauvignon Blanc;
although there is none in the blend, you would be
forgiven for believing it a posh Loire Sauvignon.

25 Júlia Florista Branco, NV
Portugal 12% **€9.95/ 7.50***

STOCKISTS:
O'Briens, obrienswine.ie

*Price when on promotion

Júlia Florista Branco, NV

TASTING NOTE
Plump apple and melon fruits with good acidity and a
rounded finish.

DRINK WITH
Perfect party wine, with or without nibbles.

STYLE
Fresh & Fruity White Wines

GRAPE VARIETY
Fernão Pires, Moscato, Albillo

BACKSTORY
This is a little sister wine of the Porta 6 range of red
Portuguese wines that have been so successful for
O'Briens. I suspect it is every bit as popular.

26 Vermentino di Sardegna 2018, Sella & Mosca
Italy 11% €14.50

STOCKISTS: Whelehan's Wines, Loughlinstown, whelehanswines.ie

Vermentino di Sardegna 2018, Sella & Mosca

TASTING NOTE
Plush rounded pineapples and melons with a hint of spice in a refreshing dangerously moreish wine.

DRINK WITH
Great before dinner or with tomato-based pasta dishes.

STYLE
Fresh & Fruity White Wines

GRAPE VARIETY
Vermentino

BACKSTORY
Vermentino, known as Rolle in Provence, is increasing in popularity with growers in warmer parts of France and Italy, where its ability to retain acidity in hot climates is prized, as well as its delicious plump fruits.

27 **Petit Chardonnay 2018,
Ken Forrester Wines,
Western Cape** South Africa
13% **€14.95** Vegan

STOCKISTS: O'Briens, obrienswine.ie

Petit Chardonnay 2018, Ken Forrester Wines, Western Cape

TASTING NOTE
A medium-bodied unoaked Chardonnay with clean ripe apple fruits and good citrus acidity. The sort of wine that grows with each sip.

DRINK WITH
This would go nicely with a variety of foods, including chicken, salmon or cheese dishes including cauliflower cheese or macaroni cheese.

STYLE
Fresh & Fruity White Wines

GRAPE VARIETY
Chardonnay

BACKSTORY
Ken Forrester is best-known for his excellent Chenin Blanc; another Forrester wine is featured on pages 99/100. However, at a recent tasting, I was also very taken by this Chardonnay.

28 Friulano 2018, Volpe Pasini, Friuli Colli Orientale Italy 12.5% €15.50

STOCKISTS:
Wines on the Green, Dublin
2, Celticwhiskeyshop.com; Blackrock Cellar, Blackrock,
blackrockcellar.com; Sweeney's D3, sweeneysd3.ie.

Friulano 2018, Volpe Pasini, Friuli Colli Orientale

TASTING NOTE
Fresh and fruity with textured rounded pears, bitter almonds, and good clean acidity.

DRINK WITH
A great aperitif, or with cold meats.

STYLE
Fresh & Fruity White Wines

GRAPE VARIETY
Friulano

BACKSTORY
Friulano, once known as Tokaji Friulano, is the 'house wine' of the Friulli-Venezia-Giula, drunk in every home and restaurant. In the right hands, it can produce seriously good wines.

29 Gambellara Classico 2018, Cantina di Gambellara
Italy 13% **€15.95** Vegan

STOCKISTS: Baggot Street Wines, Dublin 4, baggotstreetwines.com, Drinkstore, Dublin 7, drinkstore.ie; Ely Wine Store - Maynooth, Ely 64, Co Dublin, 64wine.ie; Martin's Off Licence, Dublin 3, martinsofflicence.ie; Power & Co, Lucan, power-wine.com; Red Island Wine Co. Skerries; stationtostationwine.ie; wineonline.ie.

Gambellara Classico 2018, Cantina di Gambellara

TASTING NOTE
Hints of almonds and fennel, with lemon zest and pure
thirst-quenching pear fruits.

DRINK WITH
Before dinner, with lighter fish dishes and salads.

STYLE
Fresh & Fruity White Wines

GRAPE VARIETY
Garganega

BACKSTORY
Garganega is the primary grape used to make Soave;
Gambarella lies just next door.

30 Cucú 2018, Barco del Corneta, Rueda
Spain 13.5% **€17.75**
Organic

STOCKISTS: Jus de Vine, Portmarnock, jusdevine.ie; Martin's Off Licence, Dublin 3, martinsofflicence.ie; Lilliput Stores, Dublin 7, lilliputstores.com; Green Man Wines, Dublin 6, greenmanwines.ie; Sweeney's D3, sweeneysd3.ie; Gibney's, Malahide, gibneys.com; The Corkscrew, Dublin 2, thecorkscrew.ie; Blackrock Cellar, Blackrock, blackrockcellar.com; Fallon & Byrne, Dublin 2, fallonandbyrne.com; Baggot Street Wines, Dublin 4, baggotstreetwines.com; SIYPS.com; Ely 64, Glasthule, Ely64.com.

Cucú 2018, Barco del Corneta, Rueda

TASTING NOTE
Bursting with ripe mouth-watering exotic fruits,
pineapple in particular, with a delightful cleansing
acidity. Love it.

DRINK WITH
With lighter salads, seafood or pasta with prawns or
crab.

STYLE
Fresh & Fruity White Wines

GRAPE VARIETY
Verdejo

BACKSTORY
Cucú is made by Beatriz Herranz who founded the El
Barco del Corneto estate in 2008. In a short period she
has established herself as one of the stars of the Rueda
region, making scintillating wines with real character from
the local Verdejo grape.

31 Amalaya Torrontés Riesling 2018, Calchaquí Valley
Argentina 13%
€17.99 Vegan

STOCKISTS: Baggot Street Wines, Dublin 4, baggotstreetwines.com; Blackrock Cellar, Co Dublin, blackrockcellar.com; the Corkscrew, Dublin 2, thecorkscrew.ie; Jus de Vine, Portmarnock, Co Dublin, jusdevine.ie; Kellys, Dublin 3, kellysofflicence.ie; Martin's Off-Licence, Dublin 3, martinsofflicence.ie; Michaels of Mount Merrion; Power & Co, Lucan, Power-wine.com; Red Nose Wines, Clonmel, rednosewine.com; Red Island Wine Co, Skerries, Co Dublin; wineonline.ie

Amalaya Torrontés Riesling 2018, Calchaquí Valley

TASTING NOTE
The indigenous Torrontés grape with a touch of Riesling, and it really works very well. Lightly aromatic, with subtle elderflower aromas; very fresh, crisp and pure with mouth-watering peaches, finishing dry.

DRINK WITH
By itself, or with fish. A seafood ceviche?

STYLE
Fresh & Fruity White Wines

GRAPE VARIETY
85% Torrontés, 15% Riesling

BACKSTORY
Wines made from the Torrontés grape can sometimes be a little too aromatic and rich, but in this wine, the inclusion of 15 per cent Riesling adds a lovely vibrancy to the aromas and fleshy fruit of the Torrontés. This is one of my favourite summer (and winter) white wines.

32

**Herdade dos Grous
Branco 2017, VR
Alentejo Ano**
Portugal 13% **€18**

69

STOCKISTS: Morton's, Dublin 6, mortons.ie; La Touche, Greystones, Latouchewines4u.ie; The Corkscrew, Dublin 2, thecorkscrew.ie; Fresh Outlets, freshthegoodfoodmarket.ie; Redmonds, Dublin 6; Redmonds.ie; Matson's, Grange and Bandon, matsonswinesandbeer.com; MacGuinness Wines, Dundalk, dundalkwines.com; Whelehan's Wines, Loughlinstown, whelehanswines.ie; Baggot Street Wines, Dublin 4, baggotstreetwines.com; Listons, Dublin 2, listonsfoodstore.ie; D-Six Wines, Dublin 6; peggykellys.ie; Donnybrook Fair, donnybrookfair.ie; Red Island Wine Co. Skerries.

Herdade de Grous Branco 2017, VR Alentejo Ano

TASTING NOTE
Vibrant tropical fruits with a fine seam of acidity to keep it fresh.

DRINK WITH
On its own or with rich fish dishes, such as prawns or herby fish stew.

STYLE
Fresh & Fruity White Wines

GRAPE VARIETY
Antão Vaz, Arinto, Roupeiro

BACKSTORY
Despite coming from a hot region, this wine retains a crisp freshness, thanks to the indigenous Antão Vaz and Arinto grapes both of which manage to retain acidity despite all the sunshine.

33 Terroir Único Chardonnay 2018, Viña Zorzal
Argentina 12.5% €18.50

STOCKISTS: Baggot Street Wines, Dublin 4, baggotstreetwines.com; Clontarf Wines, Dublin 3 clontarfwines.ie; La Touche, Greystones, Latouchewines4u.ie; McCambridges, Galway, Mccambridges.com; Thomas Woodberrys, Galway, Woodberrys.ie.

Terroir Único Chardonnay 2018, Viña Zorzal

TASTING NOTE
An appetising harmonious Chardonnay with mouth-watering tropical fruit, the faintest touch of spice and a clean mineral finish.

DRINK WITH
An onion tart, roast tomatoes and red peppers, a chicken salad or seafood salad.

STYLE
Fresh & Fruity White Wines

GRAPE VARIETY
Chardonnay

BACKSTORY
Juampi Michelini is making some seriously good wines at Viña Zorzal in the cool Uco Valley. See elsewhere in this book for his Malbec (pages 230/231); both wines deliver a brilliant expression of pure fresh fruit.

34

Albariño 2017, Rías Baixas, Lagar de Costa
Spain 14% **€19.95/ €16.95***

STOCKISTS: O'Briens, obrienswine.ie
*Price when on promotion.

Albariño 2017, Rías Baixas, Lagar de Costa

TASTING NOTE
A refreshing medium-bodied wine with mouth-watering pear fruits, a touch of salt, and a good crisp finish.

DRINK WITH
Drink with shellfish

STYLE
Fresh & Fruity White Wines

GRAPE VARIETY
Albariño

BACKSTORY
The vineyards where this wine is made run down to the shores of the Atlantic Ocean; is that what gives it a tantalising saline touch?

35 Clima 2016, Vale da Capucha IG Lisboa
Portugal 13.5% **€20** Organic

STOCKISTS: Lilac Wines, Dublin 3, lilacwines.ie; The Wine House, Trim; First Draft Coffee & Wine, Dublin 8, Firstdraftcoffeeandwine.com; Loose Cannon, Dublin 2, loosecanon.ie; Avoca Ballsbridge & Rathcoole, Avoca.com; Baggot Street Wines, Dublin 4, baggotstreetwines.com.

Clima 2016, Vale da Capucha IG Lisboa

TASTING NOTE
Delightful, fresh, medium-bodied white with textured ripe nectarines, and a crisp saline dry finish. Dangerously moreish.

DRINK WITH
Oily fish would be good; grilled mackerel or sardines.

STYLE
Fresh & Fruity White Wines

GRAPE VARIETY
Gouveio, Fernão Pires, Arinto

BACKSTORY
Made from a blend of three Portuguese varieties, this is one of many excellent white wines now coming out of Portugal. Vale de Capucha, run by the youthful Pedro Marques, is one of my favourite producers in Portugal for both red and white wines.

36

Reto 2018, Manchuela, Bodegas Ponce
Spain 13.5% €21
Biodynamic

STOCKISTS: The Wicklow
Wine Co., Wicklow,
wicklowwineco.ie; Jus de
Vine, Portmarnock, jusdevine.
ie; Baggot Street Wines,
Dublin 4, baggotstreetwines.
com; Blackrock Cellar,
Blackrock, blackrockcellar.
com; The Corkscrew, Dublin
2, thecorkscrew.ie; Ely
64, Glasthule, Ely64.com;
Green Man Wines, Dublin
6, greenmanwines.ie; SIYPS.
com; Martin's Off Licence, Dublin 3, martinsofflicence.ie;
Redmonds, Dublin 6; Redmonds.ie.

Reto 2018, Manchuela, Bodegas Ponce

TASTING NOTE
Delightful floral aromas leading on to a rich but refreshing palate with clean mineral lines and subtle peach fruits

DRINK WITH
By itself or with fish; a shellfish risotto?

STYLE
Fresh and fruity

GRAPE VARIETY
Albilla

BACKSTORY
Juan Antonio Ponce is something of a magician. In the baking hot arid climate of Jumilla, he somehow succeeds in producing elegant, fruity wines, including the amazing Reto. A leading proponent of biodynamic viticulture, his wines will change your mind about Monastrell, Bobal and Albilla.

37 Terlaner Cuvée 2018,
Cantina Terlan, Trentino
Italy 13.5% **€24.75**

STOCKISTS: Il Fornaio
Enoteca, Liffey Street,
Dublin 1; Ely 64, Glasthule, Ely64.com;
Worldwide Wines, Waterford, worldwidewines.ie.

Terlaner Cuvée 2018, Cantina Terlan, Trentino

TASTING NOTE
Succulent nectarines and apricots shot through with lively grapefruit and sprinkled with fresh herbs.

DRINK WITH
Try this with scallops, trout or salmon dishes.

STYLE
Fresh & Fruity White Wines

GRAPE VARIETY
Pinot Bianco 60%, Chardonnay 30%, Sauvignon Blanc 10%

BACKSTORY
A unique blend from one of the best co-operatives in Italy. Cantina Terlano has some 143 growers farming a mere 165 hectares of vines, scattered over the Dolomites mountains in the foothills of the Alps.

38

Leirana, Albariño, Forjas del Salnes 2018, Rías Baixas Spain 13% **€25**
Organic, Vegan

STOCKISTS: SEly 64, Glasthule, Ely64.com; Blackrock Cellar, Blackrock, blackrockcellar.com; Bradleys Off-licence, Cork, bradleysofflicence.ie; Loose Canon, Dublin 2, loosecanon. ie; Green Man Wines, Dublin 6, greenmanwines.ie; Red Island Wine Company, Skerries; Whelehan's Wines, Loughlinstown, whelehanswines.ie; The Corkscrew, Dublin 2, thecorkscrew.ie

Leirana, Albariño, Forjas del Salnes 2018, Rías Baixas

TASTING NOTE
Wonderful, subtle wine with plump ripe peach fruits, a touch of orange peel and lemon zest, and a wonderful saline edge.

DRINK WITH
Dublin Bay prawns with homemade lemony mayonnaise.

STYLE
Fresh & Fruity White Wines

GRAPE VARIETY
Albariño

BACKSTORY
As Rías Baixas/Albariño becomes more popular, we are seeing more small producers emerge, making some really thrilling wines that get the heart beating that little bit faster. This is one such producer.

39 Giacomo Fenocchio
Roero Arneis 2017
Italy 13.5 €26

83

STOCKISTS: Green Man Wines, Dublin 6,
greenmanwines.ie; Deveneys, D14.

Giacomo Fenocchio Roero Arneis 2017

TASTING NOTE
Nicely textured, relatively rich peach fruits with tangy slightly pithy orange peel. Soft and rounded with nice grip coming through on the finish.

DRINK WITH
Pasta with seafood - prawns or clams?

STYLE
Fresh & Fruity White Wines

GRAPE VARIETY
Chardonnay

BACKSTORY
Arneis Claudio Fenocchio makes some of the finest Barolos; I enjoyed several of these at a tasting this year, but I was also smitten by this Roero, a white wine that is far more affordable than a Barolo.

40

Adèle 2018, Côtes du Rhône Eric Texier
France 13% **€26**
Biodynamic, Vegan

STOCKISTS: Ely 64, Glasthule, Ely64.com; Baggot Street Wines, Dublin 4, baggotstreetwines.com; First Draft Coffee & Wine, Dublin 8, Firstdraftcoffeeandwine.com; Green Man Wines, Dublin 6, greenmanwines.ie;

Adèle 2018, Côtes du Rhône
Eric Texier

TASTING NOTE
Medium-bodied with vibrant fresh peaches and pears,
a clean mineral acidity and very good length. A unique
and seductive wine.

DRINK WITH
Try it with fish stew or maybe fish pasta dishes.

STYLE
Rich & Rounded White Wines

GRAPE VARIETY
Clairette

BACKSTORY
Eric Texier had no family background nor training in wine,
other than a stint working with Jean-Marie Guffens at
Verget before he began making wine in Brézème, a once
famous but forgotten region in the Northern Rhône. In a
short period, he has earned an enviable reputation.

41

Pietradolce Etna Bianco 2018
Italy 13% **€27**

STOCKISTS: Green Man Wines, Dublin 6, greenmanwines.ie.

Pietradolce Etna Bianco 2018

TASTING NOTE
An elegant, refined and delicious light white with cool green fruits, mouth-watering lemon zest, and a long dry finish.

DRINK WITH
Grilled white fish with lemon and herbs.

STYLE
Rich & Rounded White Wines

GRAPE VARIETY
Catarratto

BACKSTORY
The brooding volcanic Mount Etna produces some excellent red wine wines; the whites are less well-known but can be equally good.

42
69 Arrobas 2017, Rías Baixas, Bodegas Albamar
Spain 13% **€34**

89

STOCKISTS: Ely 64, Glasthule, Ely64.com; Green Man Wines, Dublin 6, greenmanwines.ie.

69 Arrobas 2017, Rías Baixas, Bodegas Albamar

TASTING NOTE
This was one of the best white wines I tasted in 2019. Exquisite floral aromas of honeysuckle and white flowers. Luscious pears and zesty lemon, with a saline mineral core.

DRINK WITH
Warm poached lobster with sinful quantities of garlic butter.

STYLE
Rich & Rounded White Wines

GRAPE VARIETY
Albariño

BACKSTORY
The basic Albamar (€21 – 22, independents) is a favourite but this wine, made from the oldest vines in four tiny granitic vineyards, is sensational.

43

St. Joseph 'Grand Duc du Monteillet' 2017, Domaine du Monteillet
France 13% **€38**

91

STOCKISTS: Searsons, Monkstown, searsons.com; Baggot Street Wines, Baggot St., baggotstreetwines.com.

St. Joseph 'Grand Duc du Monteillet' 2017, Domaine du Monteillet

TASTING NOTE
The Montez Les Hautes du Monteillet (€24.95) is very good, but this is superb; fresh and intensely floral with lightly textured plump rounded stone fruits, subtle nuts and a long finish.

DRINK WITH
With prawns, scallops or brill, simply grilled.

STYLE
Rich & Rounded White Wines

GRAPE VARIETY
58% Marsanne 42% Roussanne

BACKSTORY
Best known for his impressive red wines, Stéphane Montez produces some brilliant white wines, including a Condrieu and this enchanting St. Joseph.

RICH AND ROUNDED WHITE WINES

44 Réserve de Boulas Laudun Côtes du Rhône Villages 2018
France 14% €13.30
Organic

95

STOCKISTS: Marks & Spencer, Marksandspencer.com

Réserve de Boulas Laudun Côtes du Rhône Villages 2018

TASTING NOTE
Very stylish rich rounded creamy peaches backed up by a cleansing acidity. A very appealing wine with a real personality.

DRINK WITH
Richer fish dishes such as creamy fish pie, or grilled chicken.

STYLE
Rich & Rounded White Wines

GRAPE VARIETY
33% Grenache Blanc, 34% Clairette, 19% Viognier, 9% Roussanne, 5% Bourbelenc, Marsanne & Ugni Blanc.

BACKSTORY
On a visit to the Southern Rhône earlier this year, I came across a bevy of interesting white wines; cooler areas, such as Laudun can produce succulent textured wines with a cool touch.

45 d'Arenberg Hermit Crab 2016, Mclaren Vale
Australia 13% €16.95

STOCKISTS: Donnybrook Fair, donnybrookfair.ie; Deveney's, D14; Grapevine, Dalkey, onthegrapevine. ie; Shiel's, Malahide; Kellys, Dublin 3, kellysofflicence.ie; Martin's Off Licence, Dublin 3, martinsofflicence.ie; The Malt House, Trim; La Touche, Greystones, Latouchewines4u. ie; Egan's, Drogheda; 1601 Off-licence, Kinsale; Bradleys Off-licence, Cork, bradleysofflicence. ie; Morton's, Dublin 6, mortons.ie; O'Donovan's, Cork, Odonovansofflicence.com.

d'Arenberg Hermit Crab 2016, Mclaren Vale

TASTING NOTE
A delightful wine stuffed with textured apricots, peaches, cantaloupe and ginger, finishing on a dry, refreshing note.

DRINK WITH
This would be great with herby, spicy Asian seafood dishes; Vietnamese prawn salad?

STYLE
Rich & Rounded White Wines

GRAPE VARIETY
70% Viognier, 30% Marsanne

BACKSTORY
d'Arenberg produces a string of excellent wines from the McLaren Vale in South Australia; I love the succulent white wines, always fresh, and always brimming with fruit.

46

Old Vine Reserve Chenin Blanc 2018, Ken Forrester Vineyards, Stellenbosch, Vegan
South Africa 13.5% **€17.95**

99

STOCKISTS: O'Briens, obrienswine.ie

Old Vine Reserve Chenin Blanc 2018, Ken Forrester Vineyards, Stellenbosch

TASTING NOTE
Medium to full-bodied with textured creamy peaches and apricots, a touch of spice and good cleansing acidity.

DRINK WITH
Great with mild creamy curries; sweet potato, chicken korma or Cape Malay chicken curry.

STYLE
Rich & Rounded White Wines

GRAPE VARIETY
Chenin Blanc

BACKSTORY
Ken Forrester is one of the acknowledged masters of Chenin Blanc in South Africa, a country that has no shortage of this variety - at the moment just under 20% of all plantings are Chenin or Steen as it is known locally. Styles very but there are some excellent wines.

47 Quinta de Saes Tobias
Encruzado, Dão 2018
Portgual 12.5% **€18.95**
Organic not certified. Vegan

STOCKISTS: Green Man Wines,
Dublin 6, greenmanwines.
ie; Clontarf Wines, Dublin 3
clontarfwines.ie; Kellys, Dublin 3, kellysofflicence.ie; Crafted,
Bennettsbridge Kilkenny; Deveney's D14.

Quinta de Saes Tobias Encruzado, Dão 2018

TASTING NOTE
Rich cool green fruits, with subtle toasted almonds. A lovely balanced characterful dry white wine with a lightly grippy finish.

DRINK WITH
Grilled oily fish; mackerel, sardines or salmon.

STYLE
Rich & Rounded White Wines

GRAPE VARIETY
Encruzado

BACKSTORY
Encruzado is one of (many) grape varieties native to Portugal. It is responsible for some of the country's finest white wines; structured and balanced with the ability to age.

48 **Viré-Clessé 2017, Les Pierres Blanches, Domaine André Bonhomme** France 13.5%
€22.95 Organic

LES PIERRES BLANCHES
2017
GRAND VIN DE BOURGOGNE
Viré Clessé
APPELLATION VIRÉ CLESSÉ CONTRÔLÉE

MIS EN BOUTEILLE A LA PROPRIÉTÉ

Domaine André Bonhomme
Depuis 1956

PROPRIÉTAIRE - RÉCOLTANT A VIRÉ (S.-A-L.) FRANCE
PRODUCE OF FRANCE

STOCKISTS: Le Caveau, Kilkenny, lecaveau.ie; Mitchell & Sons; Listons, Dublin 2, listonsfoodstore.ie; Station to Station Wines; Blackrock Cellar, Blackrock, blackrockcellar.com; MacGuinness Wines, Dundalk, dundalkwines.com.

Viré-Clessé 2017, Les Pierres Blanches, Domaine André Bonhomme

TASTING NOTE
Gorgeous, generous, textured apple and pear fruits with a reviving crisp mineral streak, finishing dry. Lovely pure unoaked Chardonnay

DRINK WITH
This would go nicely with chicken dishes – either roast or in a creamy tarragon sauce.

STYLE
Rich & Rounded White Wines

GRAPE VARIETY
Chardonnay

BACKSTORY
I have been a fan of the Bonhomme wines for many years; they drink well when young and can also age very impressively. In the sea of indifferent wines found in the Mâconnais, they stand out as special – and are very well priced given the quality.

49 Zèphyr 2017, Les Deux Cols, Côtes du Rhône
France 13.5% **€22.95**

Les Deux Cols

Zéphyr • 2017

STOCKISTS: Searsons,
Monkstown, searsons.
com; Deveney's, Dundrum;
Martin's Off Licence, Dublin
3, martinsofflicence.ie; Ely 64,
Glasthule, Ely64.com;
Ely Wine Store, Maynooth; elywinebar.ie.

Zèphyr 2017, Les Deux Cols, Côtes du Rhône

TASTING NOTE
This is quite gorgeous and worth every cent. Honey and honeysuckle aromas; medium-bodied, textured with opulent pear fruits, a touch of toasted almonds and marzipan with a glorious finish.

DRINK WITH
Creamy mushrooms - with pasta, a risotto, or simply on sourdough toast.

STYLE
Rich & Rounded White Wines

GRAPE VARIETY
Roussanne

BACKSTORY
Roussanne is widely grown in the Rhône valley, where it is often blended with Marsanne. This example has a small percentage of Ugni Blanc to add freshness and acidity.

50

**Terrasse 2017,
Keermont,
Stellenbosch** South Africa
13.5% **€30** Vegan

STOCKISTS: The Corkscrew, Dublin 2, thecorkscrew.ie;
SIYPS.com

Terrasse 2017, Keermont, Stellenbosch

TASTING NOTE
Rich textured honey and red apples, with floral aromas and a crisp dry finish.

DRINK WITH
Mildly spicy chicken or a rich fish dish; salmon with a hollandaise sauce.

STYLE
Rich & Rounded White Wines

GRAPE VARIETY
Chenin Blanc, Sauvignon Blanc, Chardonnay, Viognier

BACKSTORY
Made primarily from a block of old Chenin Blanc, this very unusual blend works really well, with each grape adding something to the mix; the richness from the Chenin and the Viognier, the aromas and freshness from the Sauvignon Blanc, the broad apple fruit from the Chardonnay.

51

**Kumeu River Estate
Chardonnay 2018,
Auckland**
New Zealand 14% **€33**

STOCKISTS: Morton's, Dublin 6, mortons.ie;
The Corkscrew, Dublin 2, thecorkscrew.ie.

Kumeu River Estate Chardonnay 2018, Auckland

TASTING NOTE
A really impressive Chardonnay, with intense peach and pear fruits overlaid with subtle toast, and held together by a seam of crisp citrus acidity.

DRINK WITH
A seafood risotto or pastas dishes.

STYLE
Rich & Rounded White Wines

GRAPE VARIETY
Chardonnay

BACKSTORY
This is the third year in a row that we have featured a Kumeu wine. Based near Auckland, Michael Brajkovich and his family make some of the finest New World Chardonnay that often outshine the finest white Burgundy in blind tastings.

52 Arbois 'Cuvée d'Automne' Domaine de la Pinte 2016
France 13.5% €33.50
Biodynamic

STOCKISTS: Sheridan's Cheesemongers, Dublin 2, Kells, Co. Meath, Galway, sheridanscheesemongers.com; SYPS.com

Arbois 'Cuvée d'Automne' Domaine de la Pinte 2016

TASTING NOTE
Crisp and dry with wonderful waxy dried fruits, pineapples and green almonds. A great introduction to the sherry-like Vins Jaunes of the Jura.

DRINK WITH
Grilled fish, chicken dishes - the classic poulet au vin jaune with morels?

STYLE
Rich & Rounded White Wines

GRAPE VARIETY
Savagnin, Chardonnay

BACKSTORY
Made in a slightly oxidative style, with a proportion of Savagnin 'sous voile', this is a fascinating and complex wine from the Jura.

53
Clos de Saint Yves 2016, Savennières, Domaine des Baumard
France 13% **€36.75**

STOCKISTS: Searsons, Monkstown, searsons.com; Ely 64, Glasthule, Ely64.com; Ely Wine Store, Maynooth; elywinebar.ie.

Clos de Saint Yves 2016 Savennières, Domaine des Baumard

TASTING NOTE
A gloriously opulent wine with honeyed peaches and pears, a strong mineral backbone and a dry finish; this will last and improve for years to come.

DRINK WITH
Try with salmon and trout dishes, or seared scallops.

STYLE
Rich & Rounded White Wines

GRAPE VARIETY
Chenin Blanc

BACKSTORY
Florent Baumard makes a series of scintillating wines, mostly Chenin Blanc, some dry, others sweet, from his vineyards in the Loire Valley.

54

Kershaw Clonal Selection Elgin Chardonnay 2017
South Africa 13.5% **€54**
Vegan

STOCKISTS: Ely 64, Glasthule, Ely64.com; Whelehans, Loughlinstown, whelehanswines.ie; The Corkscrew, Dublin 2, thecorkscrew.ie; Mitchell & Son, Dublin 1, Sandycove, and Avoca, Ballsbridge, Kilmacanogue & Dunboyne, mitchellandson.com.

Kershaw Clonal Selection Elgin Chardonnay 2017

TASTING NOTE
A superb Chardonnay, with delectable subtle peaches and apples and a well-integrated toastiness; very linear and fresh with a mineral succulence, finishing long and dry.

DRINK WITH
A plain roast chicken, grilled turbot or black sole, with a buttery lemony sauce.

STYLE
Rich & Rounded White Wines

GRAPE VARIETY
Chardonnay

BACKSTORY
A former chef who fell in love with wine, Englishman Richard Kershaw settled in cool climate Elgin, where he produces sublime Chardonnays as well as a supremely elegant Syrah.

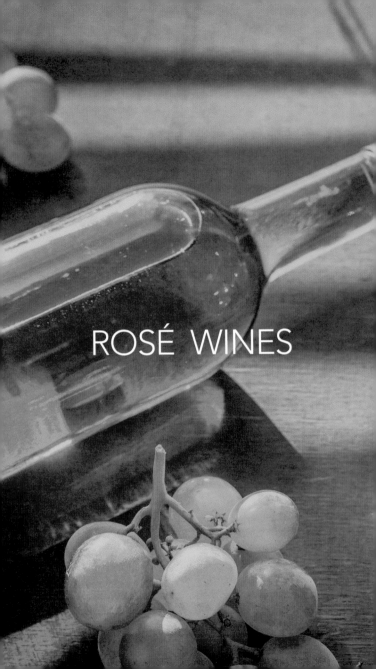

ROSÉ WINES

55

Domaine Bastide Neuve 2018, Rosé d'Oc France 12.5% €10.50

GRENACHE CINSAULT
2018

DOMAINE
BASTIDE
NEUVE

PRODUIT DE FRANCE | Rosé d'Oc
BONFILS PROPRIÉTAIRE RÉCOLTANT

STOCKISTS: Dunnes Stores, Dunnesstores.com.

Domaine Bastide Neuve 2018, Rosé d'Oc

TASTING NOTE
Light lively strawberry and late summer fruits, finishing dry. A Provencal-style rosé without the lofty price.

DRINK WITH
Perfect party wine, with or without nibbles.

STYLE
Rosé

GRAPE VARIETY
Grenache, Cinsault

BACKSTORY
We think of rosé as a summer wine, yet, like a white wine, there is no reason not to drink it all year round. If you want to make a real splash, some branches of Dunnes Stores stock this wine in magnums.

56

**Réserve du Boulas
Côtes du Rhône Rosé
2018**
France 13% **€13.30**

STOCKISTS: Marks & Spencer, Marksandspencer.com

Réserve du Boulas Côtes du Rhône Rosé 2018

TASTING NOTE
Fresh, light, clean raspberry fruits, with an attractive bright mineral edge. A very elegant and enjoyable rosé at a great price.

DRINK WITH
Try it with Salade Niçoise and other salads.

STYLE
Rosé

GRAPE VARIETY
85% Grenache, 6% Syrah, 4% Cinsault, 5% Carignan.

BACKSTORY
Fruit-filled rosés from the Southern Rhône make fantastic partners for all kinds of food; there are few things better with a table of mixed salads, vegetables and meats.

57

Ahearne Rosine Hvar
2017 Croatia 11%
€38.99 Vegan

STOCKISTS: Redmonds, Dublin 6; Redmonds.ie;
Stationtostationwine.ie.

Ahearne Rosine Hvar 2017

TASTING NOTE
Delightful rose petal aromas, light delicate tangy rosehips, a trace of grippy tannin and a gorgeous savoury note. An utterly enchanting, fascinating wine.

DRINK WITH
Grilled fish with fresh herbs.

STYLE
Rosé

GRAPE VARIETY
100% Darnekuša

BACKSTORY
Drnekuša or Darnekuša, is a very rare grape only found on the Croatian island of Hvar. Former Marks & Spencer wine buyer Jo Ahearne MW produced this unique and fascinating rosé (or is it orange?) wine.

LIGHT & ELEGANT REDS

58

Château Roc de Villepreux 2016, Bordeaux Supérieur
France 13.5% **€10.50**
Organic

STOCKISTS: Dunnes Stores, dunnesstores.com

Château Roc de Villepreux 2016, Bordeaux Supérieur

TASTING NOTE
Light, smooth, easy red fruits with an attractive herbaceous edge. Affordable everyday Bordeaux.

DRINK WITH
This would be great with grilled lamb chops served with roasted peppers - peppers are great with Cabernet Sauvignon, as is lamb.

STYLE
Light & Elegant Red Wines

GRAPE VARIETY
Merlot, Cabernet Sauvignon

BACKSTORY
At the top end Bordeaux produces some of the finest - and most expensive - wines in the world. But that represents a tiny part of total production. The rest is made up of small farmers producing lightly fruity wines, with good acidity and a dryness on the finish. They can, like this wine, offer great value for money.

59

Wildflower Pinot Noir
2018 Romania 12.5%
€13.95/€8.35* Vegan

129

STOCKISTS: O'Briens, obrienswine.ie

*Price when on promotion

Wildflower Pinot Noir 2018

TASTING NOTE
Light, easy, juicy Pinot Noir with clean cherry and blackberry fruits.

DRINK WITH
A great party wine with or without nibbles, or with grilled salmon.

STYLE
Light & Elegant Red Wines

GRAPE VARIETY
Pinot Noir

BACKSTORY
Most Pinot Noir from Romania offers great value for money; light and juicy with plenty of fruit, they are hard to beat on price.

60

**Pinot Noir 2018,
Domaine de la Renne,
Val de Loire**
France 12% **€14.15**

STOCKISTS: Wines Direct, Mullingar, and Arnott's, Dublin 1,
winesdirect.ie

Pinot Noir 2018, Domaine de la Renne, Val de Loire

TASTING NOTE
This is a delicious summer red, light and juicy with crunchy red fruits. Gouleyant, as the French would say, or very gluggable in English.

DRINK WITH
We drank this with pan-fried hake, new potatoes and the very last of the season's asparagus. Salmon or tuna would also work very well.

STYLE
Light & Elegant Red Wines

GRAPE VARIETY
Pinot Noir

BACKSTORY
Loire Pinot has been improving steadily in recent years, possibly partly due to climate change, but also as a result of better viticulture and winemaking. It also helps that our tastes have shifted a little towards lighter wines.

61 Mitchell & Son Claret
2015, Bordeau Supérieur
France 13.5% **€15**

STOCKISTS: Mitchell & Son,
Dublin 1, Sandycove, and Avoca,
Kilmacanogue & Dunboyne,
mitchellandson.com; Myles Doyle,Gorey; Wilde & Green, Dublin 6,
wildeandgreen.com. O'Driscolls Off Licence, Co. Kerry.

Mitchell & Son Claret 2015, Bordeaux Supérieur

TASTING NOTE
A very attractive well-priced Bordeaux with plenty of elegant ripe blackcurrants and cherries with ripe tannins and a pleasing soft finish.

DRINK WITH
Serve with the Sunday roast - lamb, beef or chicken.

STYLE
Light & Elegant Red Wines

134

GRAPE VARIETY
60% Merlot; 20% Cabernet Sauvignon, 20% Cabernet Franc

BACKSTORY
This is a new label and a new blend of Mitchell's Claret, a red Bordeaux blend made in consultation with Bordeaux négociant Sichel. Very good value for money

62

**Rosso Piceno 2017,
Saladini Pilastri**
Italy 13% €15.95
Organic, Vegan

ROSSO PICENO
DENOMINAZIONE DI ORIGINE CONTROLLATA

2017
SALADINI PILASTRI

STOCKISTS: Drinkstore,
Manor St., D7, drinkstore.ie;
Avoca Rathcoole & Ballsbridge,
Avoca.com; Mortons of Galway,
Mortonsofgalway.ie; Red Island
Wine Co. Skerries; 1601 Off-
licence, Kinsale; Listons, Dublin 2,
listonsfoodstore.ie; Green Man
Wines, Dublin 6, greenmanwines.ie; White Gables, Moycullen,
Co. Galway, whitegables.com.

Rosso Piceno 2017, Saladini Pilastri

TASTING NOTE
Seductive, smooth, elegant red with toothsome red cherry fruits, a touch of spice and a dry finish. Great value for money.

DRINK WITH
With roast pork or chicken.

STYLE
Light & Elegant Red Wines

GRAPE VARIETY
Montepulciano, Sangiovese

BACKSTORY
This is one of those fail-safe wines that every restaurant should stock; not too expensive and a good match for a wide variety of foods.

63 Marzemino 2018 Roberta Fugatti, IGT Marzemino della Vallagarina
Italy 13% €16 Organic

STOCKISTS: SIYPS.com;
Sheridan's Cheesemongers,
South Anne Street, Kells,
Co. Meath, Galway,
sheridanscheesemongers.com; Ely 64, Glasthule, Ely64.com;
Green Man Wines, Dublin 6, greenmanwines.ie.

Marzemino 2018 Roberta Fugatti, IGT Marzemino della Vallagarina

TASTING NOTE
Delicate aromas of violets, light juicy dark fruits, good acidity and a tannin-free finish. White wine pretending to be red? A delicious, inviting wine.

DRINK WITH
Serve cool with charcuterie and cheese.

STYLE
Light & Elegant Red Wines

GRAPE VARIETY
Marzemino

BACKSTORY
Marzemino is found mainly in the area to the south of Trentino. Its main claim to fame is a mention in Mozart's Don Giovanni!

64

Beaujolais '69' 2017, Christophe Coquard
France 12% **€16**

STOCKISTS: Grapevine, Dalkey, onthegrapevine.ie; First Draft Coffee & Wine, Dublin 8, Firstdraftcoffeeandwine.com; stationtostationwine.com; The Coach House, Dublin 16, thecoachhouseofflicence.ie; The Vintry, Dublin 6, vintry.ie

Beaujolais '69' 2017, Christophe Coquard

TASTING NOTE
Lip-smacking and light with good acidity and bouncy dark cherry fruits. Thirst-quenching Beaujolais the way it should be.

DRINK WITH
Arm yourself with a crusty baguette, some quality charcuterie, a hunk of cheese and enjoy with a cool glass of this Beaujolais.

STYLE
Light & Elegant Red Wines

GRAPE VARIETY
Gamay

BACKSTORY
Beaujolais has made a welcome comeback in recent years. Most shops now have a decent selection of these fruit-filled, tannin-free, seductive wines. The 69 in the wines title refers to winemaker Christophe Coquard's date of birth.

65

Colle Morino 2017, Barba, Montepulciano d'Abruzzo
Italy 12.5% **€16.50**

STOCKISTS:
Sheridan's Cheesemongers, Dublin 2, Kells, Co. Meath, Galway, sheridanscheesemongers.com; SYPS.com; Ely 64, Glasthule, Ely64.com.

Colle Morino 2017, Barba, Montepulciano d'Abruzzo

TASTING NOTE
Fresh, light, easy-going supple red cherry and damson fruits, without a tannin in sight. This has a lovely purity of fruit and is instantly gluggable.

DRINK WITH
Great all-purpose wine to go with lighter red meats, most white meats and hard cheeses too. Perfect pizza wine too!

STYLE
Light & Elegant Red Wines

GRAPE VARIETY
Montepulciano d'Abruzzo

BACKSTORY
This is one of my favourite wines from the Abruzzo; too many of the cheaper versions are confected and nasty. The Barba estate covers a massive 680 hectares, 130 of which are used for wine, the rest for olives, cattle, timber, and other fruits.

66

Le Vin est une Fête 2017, Côtes du Marmandais, Elian da Ros France 12.5% **€16.95** Biodynamic

Le Vin est une Fête 2017, Côtes du Marmandais, Elian da Ros

TASTING NOTE
This is another one of my all-time favourites, a subtle softly fruity wine with red berries and damsons, all in perfect balance. Cracking value for money too.

DRINK WITH
Great with roast chicken or pork, charcuterie and salads.

STYLE
Light & Elegant Reds

144

GRAPE VARIETY
40% Abouriou, 40% Cabernet Franc, 20% Merlot

BACKSTORY
Elian da Ros has virtually reinvented the Marmandais appellation over the past two decades, producing a series of high-quality wines, from, amongst others, the local Abouriou grape.

67

La Roncière Pinot Noir 2017, Val de Loire, André Vatan
France 12.5% **€17**

145

2017

La Roncière

PINOT NOIR

VAL DE LOIRE

VATAN
Arielle

INDICATION GÉOGRAPHIQUE PROTÉGÉE
MISE EN BOUTEILLE AU DOMAINE
CHAUDOUX - 18300 VERDIGNY CHER FRANCE
12%vol   PRODUIT DE FRANCE   750ml
CONTAINS SULPHITES - CONTIENT SULFITES

STOCKISTS: Whelehan's Wines, Loughlinstown, whelehanswines.ie

La Roncière Pinot Noir 2017, Val de Loire, André Vatan

TASTING NOTE
Very seductive soft sweet ripe strawberry and red cherry fruits; delicious by itself or with food. The Sancerre Rouge (€24.50) from the same producer is even better.

DRINK WITH
Salmon mayonnaise.

STYLE
Light & Elegant Reds

GRAPE VARIETY
Pinot Noir

BACKSTORY
The best (and most expensive) Pinot Noirs of the Loire come from Sancerre, but many shops also stock a less expensive Val de Loire. Some can be very good.

68

Quinta de Saes Tobias Tinto, Dão 2016
Chile 13% **€18.95**
Organic not certified.
Vegan.

STOCKISTS: Green Man Wines, Dublin 6, greenmanwines. ie; Clontarf Wines, Dublin 3 clontarfwines.ie; Kellys, Dublin 3, kellysofflicence.ie; Crafted, Bennettsbridge Kilkenny; Deveney's D14.

Quinta de Saes Tobias Tinto, Dão 2016

TASTING NOTE
Classic Dão flavours of sweet/sour dark cherries, blackberries and damsons. A very moreish refreshing red wine.

DRINK WITH
Porchetta or roast pork.

STYLE
Light & Elegant Reds

GRAPE VARIETY
25% Tinta Roriz, 25% Touriga Nacional, 25% Alfrocheiro, 25% Jaen

BACKSTORY
Dão is one of Portugal's great wine regions, but is not well known outside of the country. A relatively cool area, it produces inviting fresh mineral wines, both red and white, with a lovely purity of fruit.

69 **Tolloy Blauburgunder / Pinot Nero 2017 Sudtirol-Alto Adige** **2016** Italy 13% **€18.95**

TOLLOY

BLAUBURGUNDER
PINOT NERO

SÜDTIROL - ALTO ADIGE
DENOMINAZIONE DI ORIGINE CONTROLLATA

Kellerei Salurn

2017

STOCKISTS: Mitchell & Son, Dublin 1, Sandycove, and Avoca, Kilmacanogue & Dunboyne, mitchellandson.com.

Tolloy Blauburgunder / Pinot Nero 2017 Sudtirol-Alto Adige

TASTING NOTE
This is very gluggable light wine with piquant dark cherry fruits; a great summer or party wine.

DRINK WITH
By itself, with nibbles, or with seared salmon or tuna.

STYLE
Light & Elegant Reds

GRAPE VARIETY
Pinot Noir

BACKSTORY
Although Alto Adige is best-known for producing some of Italy's finest white wines, it also has a long tradition producing tasty light reds too. Pinot Noir is known as Pinot Nero in Italy, Blauburgunder in Austria and Switzerland.

70

Fleurie Tradition 2017, Domaine de la Madone
France 13% **€20.95**

STOCKISTS: Mitchell & Son, chq, Sandycove, and Avoca, Kilmacanogue & Dunboyne, mitchellandson.com; Myles Doyle, Gorey; Wilde & Green, Dublin 6; The Wine House, Trim.

Fleurie Tradition 2017, Domaine de la Madone

TASTING NOTE
Delicious, fresh, thirst-quenching wine with juicy dark cherry fruits, and no real tannins. Instantly gluggable.

DRINK WITH
Serve cool with charcuterie, salads and crusty sourdough.

STYLE
Light & Elegant Reds

GRAPE VARIETY
Gamay

BACKSTORY
This is lighter than some of the other Beaujolais Cru included in *WoW 2020*, but it is no less attractive, and offers great value for money.

71

di Gino 2017, Rosso Piceno San Lorenzo
Italy 13% **€21.50** Biodynamic

STOCKISTS: Sheridan's Cheesemongers, South Anne Street, Kells, Co. Meath, Galway, sheridanscheesemongers.com; Morton's, Ranelagh, mortons.ie; Green Man Wines, Terenure, greenmanwines.ie; SIYPS.com; Eleven Deli, Greystones, Elevendeli.ie.

di Gino 2017, Rosso Piceno San Lorenzo

TASTING NOTE
A charming, elegant, fragrant wine, with delicious juicy dark cherry fruits and very mild tannins.

DRINK WITH
Lighter pasta dishes – Cacio e Pepe?

STYLE
Light & Elegant Reds

GRAPE VARIETY
60% Montepulciano, 40% Sangiovese

BACKSTORY
A third-generation family estate best known for excellent Verdicchio, but the red wines are very good too.

72

Pinot Noir Les Petits Apôtres 2018, Domaine de Bon Augure
France 13% €22
Biodynamic

55

STOCKISTS: Cabot and Co., Westport, Cabotandco.com; Grapevine, Dalkey, onthegrapevine.ie; No.1 Pery Square, Limerick, Oneperysquare.com.

Pinot Noir Les Petits Apôtres 2018, Domaine de Bon Augure

TASTING NOTE
A delightful light, pure, delicate Pinot with a slight earthiness and vibrant crunchy dark cherries. Piquant and very delicious, this opened up beautifully over the course of an evening.

DRINK WITH
Feathered birds of all kinds; turkey, chicken or duck.

STYLE
Light & Elegant Reds

15

GRAPE VARIETY
Pinot Noir

BACKSTORY
Some of the cooler, high altitude parts of the Languedoc are starting to produce some seriously good Pinot Noir; this one blew me away one September evening.

73

Domaine Lardy Moulin-à-Vent Vieilles Vignes
2016 France 12.5% **€22**

57

STOCKISTS: Searsons, Monkstown, searsons.com; Mortons of Galway, Mortonsofgalway.ie; Daly's, Boyle, Co. Roscommon; Martin's Off Licence, Dublin 3, martinsofflicence.ie; D-Six Wines, Dublin 6; peggykellys.ie; The Coach House, Dublin 16, thecoachhouseofflicence.ie; Red Island Wine Co. Skerries; Thomas's of Foxrock, Thomasoffoxrock.ie; Grapevine, Dalkey, onthegrapevine.ie.

Domaine Lardy Moulin-à-Vent Vieilles Vignes 2016

TASTING NOTE
A perfume of refined strawberry fruits with freshly cut hay; the palate has good acidity and the fruit is seductively succulent.

DRINK WITH
With seared salmon or tuna..

STYLE
Light & Elegant Reds

GRAPE VARIETY
Gamay

BACKSTORY
Moulin-à-Vent is generally seen as producing the most structured long-lived wines of Beaujolais. However, this wine, made from 45-year-old vines, is very forward and dangerously easy to drink.

74

Volcánico País 2018, A los Viñateros Bravos, Itata Chile 12.5%
€23.85 Organic/Natural

59

STOCKISTS: Blackrock Cellar, Blackrock, blackrockcellar. com; Green Man Wines, Terenure, greenmanwines. ie; Fallon & Byrne, Exchequer St., fallonandbyrne.com; The Corkscrew, Chatham St., thecorkscrew.ie; Le Caveau, Kilkenny, lecaveau.ie.

Volcánico País 2018, A los Viñateros Bravos, Itata

TASTING NOTE
Light and juicy, with captivating dark fruits, an earthy, herbal touch, and fine grippy tannins on the finish.

DRINK WITH
With posh sausages served with green lentils.

STYLE
Light & Elegant Reds

GRAPE VARIETY
País

BACKSTORY
I met Leonardo Erazo in Argentina earlier this year, where he works as winemaker at Altos Las Hormigas, along with Pedro Parra (who has several other wines in this book). Erazo is a modest and unassuming man, but is obviously very knowledgeable. He also makes wine in his native Chile, in Itata, the deep south of the country, and a source of some of the country's most interesting wines. His are no exception.

75

Bourgueil 2017 La Coudraye, Y. Amirault
France 13% **€24** Organic

STOCKISTS: Sheridan's Cheesemongers, Dublin 2, Kells, Co. Meath, Galway, sheridanscheesemongers.com; Green Man Wines, Dublin 6, greenmanwines.ie; Red Nose Wines, Clonmel, rednosewine. com; Fallon & Byrne, Rathmines, fallonandbyrne.com.

Y.AMIRAULT

BOURGUEIL
APPELLATION BOURGUEIL CONTRÔLÉE

LA COUDRAYE 2017

Bourgueil 2017 La Coudraye, Y. Amirault

TASTING NOTE
Abundant blackcurrants and other dark ripe fruits, with light tannins on the impressive finish. A charming wine.

DRINK WITH
With pork chops or a firm sheep's cheese such as Cáis na Tíre or Cratloe Hills.

STYLE
Light & Elegant Reds

GRAPE VARIETY
Cabernet Franc

BACKSTORY
This is one of a brace of Loire Cab Francs featured in the guide this year. These thirst-quenching food-friendly wines deserve to be far more popular in this country.

76

Masetto Nero 2016, Endrizzi, Vigneti delle Dolomiti
Italy 14% **€24.95**

STOCKISTS: Il Fornaio
Enoteca, Liffey Street, Dublin 1; Worldwide Wines, Waterford,
worldwidewines.ie.

Masetto Nero 2016, Endrizzi, Vigneti delle Dolomiti

TASTING NOTE
Cool blue fruits, blackberries and subtle spice in a very appealing, stimulating medium-bodied red, finishing with a welcome dry tannic bite.

DRINK WITH
Roast or seared duck, pork chops in a mushroom sauce.

STYLE
Light & Elegant Reds

GRAPE VARIETY
Merlot, Cabernet Sauvignon, Lagrein, and Teroldego

BACKSTORY
This part of Italy is perhaps better known for its mouth-watering white wines, such as the Terlaner on page 80; however, there are some winning red wines too such as this vibrant example.

77

Freisa d'Asti Secco 2015, Tenuta Olim Bauda
Italy 13.5% **€24.95**

STOCKISTS: Mitchell & Son,
Dublin 1, Sandycove, and Avoca, Kilmacanogue & Dunboyne,
mitchellandson.com.

Freisa d'Asti Secco 2015, Tenuta Olim Bauda

TASTING NOTE
Raspberry aroma, elegant raspberry and rosehip fruits, with light drying tannins and a pleasant tartness. Different and very delicious.

DRINK WITH
It certainly needs food; a mushroom risotto or a plate of salumi.

STYLE
Light & Elegant Reds

GRAPE VARIETY
Freisa

BACKSTORY
Freisa is one of the more obscure grapes of Piemonte, and can be sweet, dry, still or lightly fizzy. This enchanting version is dry and still.

78 Drink Me Nat 'Cool'
2017, 1 litre bottle, Bairrada, Niepoort
Portugal 12% **€25** Organic

STOCKISTS: Loose Cannon, Dublin 2, loosecanon. ie; Baggot Street Wines, Dublin 2; Green Man Wines, Dublin 6, greenmanwines.ie; Higgins Off-Licence, Dublin 14, www.higginsofflicence. ie; The Corkscrew, Dublin 2, thecorkscrew.ie; First Draft Coffee & Wine, Dublin 8, Firstdraftcoffeeandwine. com; Ely 64, Glasthule, Ely64. com; Mitchell & Son, Dublin 1, Sandycove, and Avoca, Kilmacanogue & Dunboyne, mitchellandson.com.

Drink Me Nat 'Cool' 2017, 1 litre bottle, Bairrada, Niepoort

TASTING NOTE
Wild and funky with floral aromas and lively mouth-watering red fruits. Light-bodied and instantly gluggable.

DRINK WITH
Plonk it down on the table at any casual dinner - and watch it disappear.

STYLE
Light & Elegant Reds

GRAPE VARIETY
Baga

BACKSTORY
As well as being one of the great names in Port, Dirk Niepoort produces a range of fascinating wines from other parts of northern Portugal, always featuring local grape varieties. This red 'Pet Nat' or lightly sparkling red wine is yet another fine example.

79

Ch. Jean Faux Les Sources 2014, Bordeaux Supérieur
France 14% **€26** Organic

Ch. Jean Faux Les Sources 2014, Bordeaux Supérieur

TASTING NOTE

A medium-bodied wine with elegant red fruits, a spicy edge and a fine tannic grip on the finish. Bordeaux as it should be.

DRINK WITH

I drank a bottle over two evenings, once with roast chicken, the second with an autumnal mushroom risotto. Both worked really well.

STYLE

Light & Elegant Reds

GRAPE VARIETY

70% Merlot, 30% Cabernet Franc

BACKSTORY

This is classic Bordeaux; restrained, harmonious and subtle. It draws you back to the glass again and again and seems better every time.

80

Camiño Real 2017 Ribeira Sacra, Guímaro
Spain 13.5% **€26**

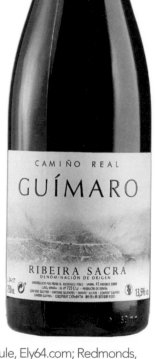

STOCKISTS: Green Man Wines, Dublin 6, greenmanwines.ie; Ely 64, Glasthule, Ely64.com; Redmonds, Dublin 6; Redmonds.ie.

Camiño Real 2017 Ribeira Sacra, Guímaro

TASTING NOTE
Lightly aromatic with seductive perfectly ripe dark cherry fruits, a spicy savoury edge and a freshness, an elegance that draws you back for another sip. Delicious wine.

DRINK WITH
A seared breast of duck, or maybe belly of pork.

STYLE
Light & Elegant Reds

GRAPE VARIETY
Mencía

BACKSTORY
Pedro Rodríguez is one of the rising stars of Ribeira Sacra, a region in Galicia that has attracted huge interest in recent years - for the amazing scenery as well as the unique wines. Made primarily from ancient Mencía vines clinging to the slate soils on vertiginous slopes sweeping down to the rivers Miño and Sil, the wines can be spectacularly good.

81

Folk Machine 'Parts & Labor' Red 2016, California
USA 12.5% **€26**
Organic

STOCKISTS:
stationtostationwine.com; First Draft Coffee & Wine, Dublin 8, Firstdraftcoffeeandwine.com; Redmonds, Dublin 6; Redmonds.ie.

Folk Machine 'Parts & Labor' Red 2016, California

TASTING NOTE
Fresh, juicy, pure damson fruits with a twist of acidity. Clean, light and tangy, this is not your typical California fruit-bomb.

DRINK WITH
I'd fancy this with a grilled salmon steak, possibly glazed with soy and miso.

STYLE
Light & Elegant Reds

GRAPE VARIETY
Syrah, Grenache, Barbera, Carignan

BACKSTORY
Made from an eclectic blend of grapes, each sourced from a different region of California, this will certainly bring out your inner wine anorak.

82 Silice 2017, Ribeira Sacra Spain
12.5% €26.95

STOCKISTS: Searsons Monkstown, searsons.com; Drinkstore, D7, drinkstore.ie.

Silice 2017, Ribeira Sacra

TASTING NOTE
Seductive, soft, sweet/sour dark cherry fruits; light, svelte and charming. One of those bottles that magically disappears.

DRINK WITH
Try this with pork dishes - pork chops with mushrooms.

STYLE
Light & Elegant Reds

GRAPE VARIETY
Mencía

BACKSTORY
Think of a cross between a cool elegant peppery Syrah from the Northern Rhône and a seductive silky Pinot Noir; you might well come up with a Mencía from Ribeira Sacra.

83

**Domaine Desvignes
Morgon 'La Voûte
St-Vincent' 2017**
France 12.5% **€27** Organic

STOCKISTS: Ely 64, Glasthule,
Ely64.com; La Touche,
Greystones, Latouchewines4u.ie;
Green Man Wines, Dublin 6, greenmanwines.ie;
Clontarf Wines, Dublin 3 clontarfwines.ie.

Domaine Desvignes Morgon 'La Voûte St-Vincent' 2017

TASTING NOTE
An utterly charming wine, fragrant and fresh, with layers of elegant ripe red fruits, but with real depth and concentration too.

DRINK WITH
Serve with roast or grilled chicken or chicken salads.

STYLE
Light & Elegant Reds

GRAPE VARIETY
Gamay

BACKSTORY
One of the finest wines from Beaujolais I have tasted this year; proof, if needed, that the top crus can compare with the very best wines.

84

Framingham Pinot Noir 2016, Marlborough
New Zealand 13.5% **€27.99**
Vegan

179

FRAMINGHAM

PINOT NOIR
2016

FRAMINGHAM
F
WINES

MARLBOROUGH

STOCKISTS: TheCorkscrew, Chatham St., thecorkscrew.ie; Green Man Wines, Terenure, greenmanwines.ie; J.J. O'Driscoll, Ballinlough, jjodriscoll.ie; Wineonline.ie; Stationtostationwine.ie.

Framingham Pinot Noir 2016, Marlborough

TASTING NOTE
Beguiling lightly smoky nose with violets and summer fruits. A complex palate with a savoury edge and light tannins to offset the vibrant dark cherry fruits.

DRINK WITH
With lamb or duck.

STYLE
Light & Elegant Reds

GRAPE VARIETY
Pinot Noir

BACKSTORY
The various Framingham Sauvignons have appeared in the book before, but this marks the Pinot's debut. About time. It is a great wine.

85

Chinon Vieilles Vignes 2017, Domaine Philippe Alliet
France 13.5% **€29.50**

STOCKISTS: Terroirs, Dublin 4, Terroirs.ie

Chinon Vieilles Vignes 2017, Domaine Philippe Alliet

TASTING NOTE
Silky and elegant with lead pencils, and juicy peppery blackcurrants; supple and easy-going. A joy to drink.

DRINK WITH
A loin of pork roasted with peppers.

STYLE
Light & Elegant Reds

GRAPE VARIETY
Tintilla

BACKSTORY
Classic Loire Cabernet Franc offers a distinctive set of flavours that I find completely irresistible; red and blackcurrants, lead pencils, a leafiness with age, and a lively edge.

86

Le Temps des C(e)rises 2014, Santenay, Domaine Olivier

France 13% **€29.95/€23.95***

183

STOCKISTS: O'Briens, obrienswine.ie
*Price when on promotion

Le Temps des C(e)rises 2014, Santenay, Domaine Olivier

TASTING NOTE
Light, piquant, juicy red cherries and developing a nose of *sous bois* or forest floor - there is a touch of Burgundian class here - a very attractive delicate mature red Burgundy.

DRINK WITH
Something subdued - poached chicken or some mild cheese.

STYLE
Light & Elegant Reds

GRAPE VARIETY
Pinot Noir

BACKSTORY
Santenay, at the very south of the Côte d'Or, is not among the best-known communes in Burgundy, and as a result can offer good value.

87

Lomba dos Ares 2016, Ribeira Sacra, Fedellos do Couto
Spain 12.5% **€31**

FEDELLOS DO COUTO

APRESENTA

LOMBA DOS ARES

2016

EMBOTELLADO EN ORIXE

STOCKISTS: Ely 64, Glasthule, Ely64.com; Green Man Wines, Terenure, greenmanwines.ie; Loose Canon, 29 Drury St., loosecanon.ie.

Lomba dos Ares 2016, Ribeira Sacra, Fedellos do Couto

TASTING NOTE
Made from a host of local grapes, mainly Mencía, this is a wonderful wine. Fragrant and floral with refined and refreshing cool dark cherry fruits, a nice grip and an impressively smooth finish.

DRINK WITH
With charcuterie of any kind or a slow-roasted belly of pork.

STYLE
Light & Elegant Reds

GRAPE VARIETY
Mencía

BACKSTORY
The Mencía grape and the Ribeira Sacra region are having a bit of a moment. There are three in WoW 2020; all have that fresh, elegant, sweet/savoury fruit that makes them so special.

88 Sancerre Rouge La Croix du Roy 2014, Lucien Crochet Vineyard France 13% €34

STOCKISTS:
SIYPS.com; Green Man Wines, Dublin 6, greenmanwines.ie; Ely 64, Glasthule, Ely64.com; Sheridan's Cheesemongers, Galway, sheridanscheesemongers.com; Mitchell & Son, Dublin 1, Sandycove, and Avoca, Kilmacanogue & Dunboyne, mitchellandson.com.

Sancerre Rouge La Croix du Roy 2014, Lucien Crochet

TASTING NOTE
Soft, fragrant, mature delicate fruits - soft cherries with a light herbal note and good acidity. A real charmer.

DRINK WITH
Perfect with warm poached salmon.

STYLE
Light & Elegant Reds

GRAPE VARIETY
Pinot Noir

BACKSTORY
Red Sancerre, always made with Pinot Noir, is generally lighter and more delicate than a red Burgundy. Sancerre can offer wonderful fragrance and exquisite refined pure fruits - as with this wine.

89

**Bourgogne Pinot Noir
2015, Sylvain Pataille**
France 13% **€35** Organic

STOCKISTS: Ely 64, Glasthule, Ely64.com.

Bourgogne Pinot Noir 2015, Sylvain Pataille

TASTING NOTE
This is a lovely glass of wine: perfumed and elegant, with pure ripe dark cherries, just enough acidity and very good concentration. I suspect this will continue to improve for a year or two, but a joy to drink right now.

DRINK WITH
Roast duck, goose or guinea fowl.

STYLE
Light & Elegant Red Wines

GRAPE VARIETY
Pinot Noir

BACKSTORY
Sylvain Pataille is based in Marsannay, one of the lesser rated parts of Burgundy. But his wines are the equal, if not better, than many more illustrious (and expensive) names.

90

**Rouge-Gorge 2017,
Coteaux du Loir
Domaine de Bellivière**
France 13% **€39**
Biodynamic

STOCKISTS: SIYPS.com; Ely
64, Glasthule, Ely64.com; Green Man Wines, Dublin 6,
greenmanwines.ie.

Rouge-Gorge 2017, Coteaux du Loir Domaine de Bellivière

TASTING NOTE

An utterly charming, lightly aromatic wine, with elegant redcurrant fruits and light tannins on the finish. It has good acidity, giving it a freshness and an attractive subtle earthiness. There is a wonderful purity of fruit that draws you back to the glass time after time. Well, it did me anyway.

DRINK WITH

We drank it with our weekly roast organic chicken, often the perfect match for any wine, red or white. Serve it very cool; I chilled ours in the fridge for half an hour. It then warmed up as we drank it.

STYLE

Light & Elegant Red Wines

GRAPE VARIETY

Pineau d'Aunis

BACKSTORY

The vineyards are farmed biodynamically. Eric Nicolas uses natural yeasts and minimal intervention in his winemaking, fermenting in large barrels in his tufa caves. That probably makes this a natural wine, although this bears little resemblance to most that I have tasted. Over the last decade, Nicolas has built a reputation as one of the finest white winemakers in the Loire Valley, crafting sublime dry, medium and sweet wines from the lesser-known appellations of Jasnières and Coteaux du Loir. Try his sublime Vieilles Vignes Eparses (€48) if you get the chance. All of the white wines are made from Chenin Blanc. Pineau d'Aunis is, as the label tells us, an unusual local red grape variety, a close relative of Chenin Blanc.

91

La Porte Saint Jean, Saumur 2015, Sylvain Dittière France 12.5%
€39.50

STOCKISTS: Terroirs, Dublin 4, Terroirs.ie

La Porte Saint Jean, Saumur 2015, Sylvain Dittière

TASTING NOTE
A superb, refined Cabernet Franc with intense ripe blackcurrants and red cherries, a touch of lead pencil, and a precise long elegant finish.

DRINK WITH
With your finest organic roast chicken.

STYLE
Light & Elegant Red Wines

GRAPE VARIETY
Cabernet Franc

BACKSTORY
I know it is not cheap, but this was one of the finest wines I have tasted over the last 12 months. Definitely worth cracking open the piggy bank.

ROUNDED AND FRUITY
RED WINES

92 Aldi Exquisite Collection Pinot Noir 2018, Wairarapa
New Zealand 13% **€9.99**

STOCKISTS: Aldi, Aldi.ie

Aldi Exquisite Collection Pinot Noir, Wairarapa

TASTING NOTE
Light, fresh and juicy with slightly earthy damson fruits.
Perfect budget Pinot Noir.

DRINK WITH
Drink solo, with salmon or lighter chicken dishes.

STYLE
Rounded & Fruity Red Wines

GRAPE VARIETY
Pinot Noir

BACKSTORY
Various regions of New Zealand produce seriously good
Pinot Noir brimming with juicy ripe fruits. This wine is an
outstanding bargain.

93 **Santa Rita 120 Cabernet Franc 2018, Central Valley** Chile 13% **€12.50**

STOCKISTS: Tesco, Tesco.ie; SuperValu, Supervalu.ie.

Santa Rita 120 Cabernet Franc, 2018 Central Valley

TASTING NOTE
Medium-bodied with herby, leafy red fruits, and some
well-integrated tannins kicking in on the finish.

DRINK WITH
A roast loin of pork with garlic and herbs.

STYLE
Rounded & Fruity Red Wines

GRAPE VARIETY
Cabernet Franc

200

BACKSTORY
Chile has been famous for its Cab Sauv for decades; here
Santa Rita try their hand with Cabernet Franc with some
success. This is great value for money.

94

Ciello Rosso 2018 IGP Terre Siciliane
Italy 12.5% **€12.95**
Organic

STOCKISTS: Avoca; Baggot Street Wines; Blackrock Cellars; Le Caveau; Bradleys Off License Cork; Clontarf Wines; Fallon and Byrne; Green Man Wines; 64 wines; World Wide Wines

Ciello Rosso 2018 IGP
Terre Siciliane

TASTING NOTE
Light, juicy ripe plum, red cherry and strawberry fruits
with a subtle earthy touch. A supple easy-drinking wine.

DRINK WITH
On its own or with pizza, focaccia or perhaps a few
arancini.

STYLE
Rounded & Fruity Red Wines

GRAPE VARIETY
Nero d'Avola

BACKSTORY
The Vesco family have 100 hectares of organically-grown
vines high up in the hills above Alcamo. Here they produce
a range of light and fresh wines in a style rarely found in
Sicily.

95

Les Vignes d'Oc Rouge Grenache / Merlot 2018, Languedoc
France 12.5% **€12.99**

STOCKISTS: Grapevine, Dalkey
onthegrapevine.ie; Cabot and Co.,
Westport, cabotandco.com;
No1. Pery Square, Limerick,
Oneperysquare.com;
The PoppySeed, Clarinbridge, poppyseed.ie. ie; McHughs,
Kilbarrack Road & Malahide Rd., mchughs.ie.

Les Vignes d'Oc Rouge Grenache / Merlot 2018, Languedoc

TASTING NOTE
Elegant, smooth, harmonious red fruits, with a soft, easy finish. Perfect mid-week drinking.

DRINK WITH
Chicken pork or tomato-based pasta dishes.

STYLE
Rounded & Fruity Red Wines

GRAPE VARIETY
Grenache, Merlot

BACKSTORY
Claude Serra, professor of Oenology (winemaking) at Montpellier University, makes this wine alongside his colleague Daniel Orsolini; together they source grapes from various parts of the Languedoc to make a range of very quaffable easy-drinking wines.

96

T'Air d'Oc Syrah, Pays d'Oc 2018, Domaine Gayda
France 13% **€14.95**

STOCKISTS: Jnwine.com;
Ely 64, Glasthule, Ely64.com; The Counter, Letterkenny,
Thecounterdeli.com; Donnybrook Fair, donnybrookfair.ie.

T'Air d'Oc Syrah, Pays d'Oc 2018, Domaine Gayda

TASTING NOTE
A very charming easy-going red with light peppery cherry fruits and a smooth finish. Very keenly priced too.

DRINK WITH
A great all-rounder with white meats, lighter red meats and game.

STYLE
Rounded & Fruity Red Wine's

GRAPE VARIETY
Syrah

BACKSTORY
A large domaine close to Carcassonne in the Languedoc. It was set up in 2004 by an Englishman, a South African and a French winemaker. With assistance from renowned South African winemaker Marc Kent, they produce a series of very well-made modern wines.

97 Rosso Piceno DOC, Cantina dei Colli Ripani 2018
Italy 13% **€14.95** Organic

STOCKISTS: Ely 64, Glasthule,
Ely64.com; Crafted, Bennettsbridge
Kilkenny; Ardkeen Quality Foodstore, Waterford, Ardkeen.com;
Kellys, Dublin 3, kellysofflicence.ie.

Rosso Piceno DOC, Cantina dei Colli Ripani 2018

TASTING NOTE
This is a very attractive easy-going inexpensive wine with supple savoury sour cherry fruits and a smooth rounded finish.

DRINK WITH
A great all-rounder; try it with pizzas or tomato-based pasta dishes.

STYLE
Rounded & Fruity Red Wines

GRAPE VARIETY
Montepulciano and Sangiovese

BACKSTORY
Rosso Piceno is part of the Marche region, next door to the better-known Abruzzo. Both white and red wines can be very good and very fairly priced. I list two reds in this edition of *WoW*.

98 Ars in Vitro 2016, Tandem, Valle de Yerri, Navarra
Spain 14% **€14.95** Vegan

STOCKISTS:
O'Briens, obrienswine.ie

Ars in Vitro 2016, Tandem, Valle de Yerri, Navarra

TASTING NOTE
Cool, clean and slightly mineral with pure plum fruits and light grippy tannins on the finish. Good wine at a great price.

DRINK WITH
A great all-rounder that would go nicely with most red and white meats, or roast Mediterranean vegetables.

STYLE
Rounded & Fruity Red Wines

GRAPE VARIETY
Tempranillo, Merlot

BACKSTORY
WoW has consistently featured wines from this small family estate. And with good reason. This year I was very taken with this unusual blend of Tempranillo and Merlot.

99 Ch. Bellevue-La-Forêt 2016, Fronton
France 13% €16
Organic not certified.

STOCKISTS: La Touche, Greystones, Latouchewines4u. ie; The Vintry, Dublin 6, vintry.ie; Morton's, Dublin 6, mortons.ie; Redmonds, Dublin 6; Redmonds. ie; D-Six Wines, Dublin 6; peggykellys.ie; Thomas's of Foxrock, thomasoffoxrock.ie; Fresh Outlets, freshthegoodfoodmarket. ie; Dunnes Stores, dunnesstores. com; Martin's Off Licence, Dublin 3, martinsofflicence.ie; Higgins, Clonskeagh, Higginsfflicence.ie; Fagan's, D9, Fagans.ie; Molloy's Liquor Stores, molloys.ie; The Vineyard, Galway; Eldon's, Clonmel; Donnybrook Fair, donnybrookfair.ie.

Ch. Bellevue-La-Forêt 2016, Fronton

TASTING NOTE
Medium-bodied with firm blackcurrants and brambly red fruits kicking in with a good tannic bite on the finish.

DRINK WITH
Macaroni cheese or lighter pork dishes - a stuffed pork steak.

STYLE
Rounded & Fruity Red Wines

GRAPE VARIETY
Negrette, Cabernet Sauvignon, Cabernet Franc

BACKSTORY
An old favourite that has appeared in earlier editions of WoW, this property has been owned by Irishman Philip Grant since 2008. Negrette is a local grape variety that has attractive peppery fruits.

100

Altos Las Hormigas Tinto 2017, Mendoza
Argentina 14%
€17.99 Vegan

STOCKISTS: Donnybrook Fair, donnybrookfair.ie; Green Man Wines, Dublin 6, greenmanwines.ie; Martin's Off Licence, Dublin 3, martinsofflicence.ie; Clontarf Wines, Dublin 3 clontarfwines.ie; Red Island Wine Co. Skerries; Ely 64, Glasthule, Ely64.com; Ely Wine Store, Maynooth; elywinebar.ie; Redmonds, Dublin 6; Redmonds.ie; Stationtostationwine.ie; The Cinnamon Cottage, Cork, cinnamoncottage.ie; The Corkscrew, Chatham St., thecorkscrew.ie; The Vintry, Dublin 6 vintry.ie; wineonline.ie.

Altos Las Hormigas Tinto 2017, Mendoza

TASTING NOTE
The blend used to make this wine includes Semillon (a white grape) which gives it a very attractive elegance. This sits well with the smooth and lively red cherry fruits and the nicely rounded tannin-free finish.

DRINK WITH
Try it with dishes featuring herby tomatoes and/or red peppers.

STYLE
Rounded & Fruity Red Wines

GRAPE VARIETY
48% Bonarda, 45% Malbec, 7% Semillon

BACKSTORY
Founded in 1995 by Tuscan winemakers Alberto Antonini and Antonio Morescalchi, since joined by others, Altos Las Hormigas is endeavouring to produce a fresher, lighter style of wine, mainly using Malbec, with less alcohol and neutral oak. The resulting wines combine power and elegance in a very seductive manner.

101

Viano 'Hillside" Red NV USA 13%
€18 Organic

STOCKISTS: Grapevine, Dalkey, onthegrapevine.ie; stationtostationwine.com; Deveney's, D14.

Viano 'Hillside" Red NV

TASTING NOTE
This wine is light in body with grippy, earthy, fresh plum fruits and a touch of spice. Californian Beaujolais?

DRINK WITH
Spicy barbecued ribs.

STYLE
Rounded & Fruity Red Wines

GRAPE VARIETY
Gamay

BACKSTORY
Traditional winemaking with grapes from a century-old vineyard in Contra Costa County makes for a very different, more traditional style of wine. Intriguing.

102

Clos des Fous "Pour ma Gueule" 2017, Itata Valley
Chile 14% **€19.99**
Vegan

STOCKISTS: Blackrock Cellar, Blackrock, blackrockcellar. com; Grapevine, Dalkey, onthegrapevine.ie; Green Man Wines, Terenure, greenmanwines.ie; Martin's Off Licence, Clontarf, martinsofflicence.ie; Stationtostationwine.ie; Wineonline.ie.

Clos des Fous "Pour ma Gueule" 2017, Itata Valley

TASTING NOTE
A very moreish lightly grippy wine with vivid crunchy fresh red berry fruits. Cleansing, uplifting wine.

DRINK WITH
By itself, with cold meats or ham with parsley sauce.

STYLE
Rounded and Fruity Red Wines

GRAPE VARIETY
76% Cinsault, 16% País, 8% Carignan

BACKSTORY
Itata, along with neighbouring Bío-Bío and Malleco, are the most southerly vineyards in Chile, as well as being the oldest. Once seen as a backwater, producing the cheapest jug wines for home consumption, Itata is now producing some of the most exciting wines in Chile. Clos des Fous was among the first to make quality wine in the region.

103

Sherazade Donnafugata 2018, Sicilia DOC, Nero d'Avola Italy 13%
€23 Vegan

STOCKISTS: Alain & Christine's, Kenmare, acwine.ie; Baggot Street Wines, Dublin 4, baggotstreetwines.com; Cashel Wine Cellar, cashel.ie; Drink Store, Dublin 7, drinkstore. ie; Ely 64, Glasthule, Ely64. com; Fallon & Byrne, Dublin 2, fallonandbyrne.com; Gibney's, Malahide, gibneys.com; Jus de Vine, Portmarnock, Co Dublin, jusdevine.ie   Martin's Off-Licence, Dublin 3, martinsofflicence.ie; Red Island Wine Co. Skerries; Redmonds of Ranelagh, redmonds.ie; Searsons, Monkstown, searsons.com; The Corkscrew, Dublin 2, thecorkscrew.ie; Thomas Woodberrys, Galway, Woodberrys.ie; Wineonline.ie.

Sherazade Donnafugata 2018, Sicilia DOC, Nero d'Avola

TASTING NOTE
A smooth mouthful of voluptuous dark fruits with hints of spice and nicely integrated tannins on the finish.

DRINK WITH
Serve cool with roast lamb accompanied by roast Mediterranean vegetables or caponata.

STYLE
Rounded and fruity red wines

GRAPE VARIETY
Nero d'Avola

BACKSTORY
Donnafugata is a family-run business producing a range of excellent wines from Sicily, as well as a stupendous sweet wine, Ben Ryé, from the neighbouring island of Pantelleria.

104

Montes Outer Limits "Old Roots" Cinsault 2018, Itata
Chile 13.5% **€23.99**
Vegan

STOCKISTS: Blackrock Cellar, Blackrock, blackrockcellar.com; Baggot Street Wines, Baggot St., baggotstreetwines.com; Dwan's Off Licence, Dublin 16; Ely Wine Store - Maynooth, Ely 64 Wine, Glasthule, 64wine.ie; Michael's, Mount Merrion, michaels.ie; Wineonline.ie.

Montes Outer Limits "Old Roots" Cinsault 2018, Itata

TASTING NOTE
Floral, with vibrant mouth-watering pure black fruits, subtle notes of spice, and a sappy dry finish.

DRINK WITH
Try this with a barbecued or roast belly of pork.

STYLE
Rounded and fruity red wines

GRAPE VARIETY
Cinsault

BACKSTORY
There are four wines from Itata in this edition of WoW; I have always been a fan, but a trip to the region earlier this year left me really impressed with the wines - and the picturesque vineyards.

105 Cuvée Equinox 2017, Crozes-Hermitage, Domaine des Lises
France 13.5% **€24**

STOCKISTS: Mitchell & Son,
Dublin 1, Sandycove, and
Avoca, Kilmacanogue & Dunboyne, mitchellandson.com;
Green Man Wines, Dublin 6, greenmanwines.ie; SIYPS.com.

Cuvée Equinox 2017, Crozes-Hermitage, Domaine des Lises

TASTING NOTE
"Our picnic wine", says winemaker Thomas Schmittel. A light, refreshing, supple wine with exuberant savoury dark cherry fruits and a tannin-free finish.

DRINK WITH
With a picnic obviously, a plate of cold meats, cheese and other deli goodies.

STYLE
Rounded and fruity red wines

GRAPE VARIETY
Syrah

BACKSTORY
Domaine des Lises is owned by the Graillot family, producers of some of the finest Syrah in the Northern Rhône.

106

Bourgogne 2017, Domaine Derey Frères
France 13% **€24.50**

225

STOCKISTS: Whelehan's Wines, Loughlinstown, wwwelehanswines.ie

Bourgogne 2017, Domaine Derey Frères

TASTING NOTE
Soft, elegant, slightly leafy rounded damson and red cherry fruits; one to enjoy now.

DRINK WITH
Salmon, chicken salad, or a roast chicken.

STYLE
Rounded and fruity red wines

GRAPE VARIETY
Pinot Noir

BACKSTORY
Pinot Noir has a healthy representation in WoW2020, including wines from New Zealand, the US and the Loire Valley. This is one of three from Burgundy, the home of this wonderful grape.

107 Johanneshöhe
Blaufränkisch 2017,
Burgenland, Prieler
Austria 13% **€25** Organic
(in conversion) and Vegan

STOCKISTS: Blackrock Cellar, Blackrock, Blackrockcellar.com;
The Corkscrew, Dublin 2, thecorkscrew.ie

Johanneshöhe Blaufränkisch 2017, Burgenland, Prieler

TASTING NOTE
Pure refined Blaufränkisch, instantly drinkable, with silky smooth dark cherry and damson fruits sprinkled with a touch of spice.

DRINK WITH
Ham, roast pork, mushroom risotto, or roast chicken.

STYLE
Rounded and fruity red wines

GRAPE VARIETY
Blaufränkisch

BACKSTORY
Last year I featured Georg Prieler's magnificent Pinot Blanc. This year it's his Blaufränkisch, a wine made from nine different iron-rich vineyards in Burgenland.

108

Eggo Tinto de Tiza Malbec 2016, Viña Zorzal

Argentina 14% **€25**

STOCKISTS: La Touche, Greystones, Latouchewines4u. ie; Green Man Wines, Terenure, greenmanwines.ie; Blackrock Cellar, Blackrock, blackrockcellar. com; Clontarf Wines, clontarfwines.ie

Eggo Tinto de Tiza Malbec 2016, Viña Zorzal

TASTING NOTE
This is a superb unoaked wine; clean and elegant, with its fresh, deep, dark loganberry fruits it might change the way you think about Malbec - for the better.

DRINK WITH
Perfect with all sorts of roast or grilled lamb.

STYLE
Rounded and fruity red wines

GRAPE VARIETY
Malbec

BACKSTORY
This wine is made in a concrete egg, all the rage these days. The egg shape gives a continuous flow to the wine and the concrete provides a steady temperature.

109

**Daniel Bouland
Morgon Courcelette
Vieilles Vignes 2016**
France 13.5% **€26**

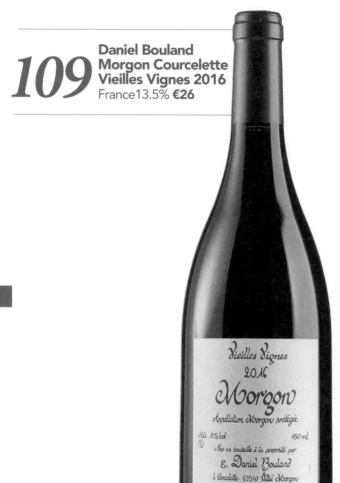

STOCKISTS: Cabot and
Co., Westport, Cabotandco.
com; Ely 64, Glasthule, Ely64.
com; No.1 Pery Square,
Limerick, Oneperysquare.com; Ely 64, Glasthule, Ely64.com;
Stationtostationwine.ie; Market 57, Westport.

Daniel Bouland Morgon Courcelette Vieilles Vignes 2016

TASTING NOTE
Elegant and refined with a seductive fragrance;
combines freshness and power in the same mouthful;
concentrated dark cherry fruits and soft, fine tannins.

DRINK WITH
Some garlicky Toulouse sausages with green lentils.

STYLE
Rounded and fruity red wines

GRAPE VARIETY
Gamay

BACKSTORY
While you can buy cru Beaujolais for a lot less than €26,
I believe this wine is worth every cent. The same wine
featured two years ago in *WoW*; it has matured perfectly.

110

**Imaginador 2017,
Pedro Parra, Itata**
Chile 14% **€26.99**

STOCKISTS: Ely Wine Store,
Maynooth, elywinebar.ie; Wineonline.ie.

Imaginador 2017, Pedro Parra, Itata

TASTING NOTE
Bright, fresh and lively with savoury dark cherry fruits, a light grippiness and a spicy twist. A wine with amazing substance, ripeness and depth.

DRINK WITH
Try it with bangers and mash or maybe grilled liver - fegato alla veneziana?

STYLE
Rounded & Fruity Red Wines

GRAPE VARIETY
Cinsault

BACKSTORY
As outlined elsewhere in this book, Itata was one of the first parts of Chile to be planted with vines. It has some of the oldest vineyards in the country. This wine is made by Pedro Parra, one of the world's foremost soil experts, in his new winery in Itata. The grapes are sourced from four vineyards, all with granite soils.

111

**Chemin des Fonts
2018, Les Deux Cols,
Côtes du Rhône**
France 14.5% **€28.50**

STOCKISTS: Searsons
Monkstown, searsons.com;
Deveney's, Dundrum; Ely 64, Glasthule, Ely64.com;
SIYPS.com.

Chemin des Fonts 2018, Les Deux Cols, Côtes du Rhône

TASTING NOTE
Refined, lifted aromas of spice, dark fruits and liquorice; the palate is silky-smooth with plum fruits, black olives and spice again. A very impressive wine.

DRINK WITH
Meatballs in a rich tomato sauce; lasagna, vegetarian or beef, or chicken thighs in a mushroom sauce

STYLE
Rounded and Fruity Red Wines

GRAPE VARIETY
80% Grenache, Carignan, Syrah

BACKSTORY
Made by a trio of Irish and adopted Irishmen in a cooler part of the Southern Rhône, this is the first release of Chemin des Fonts. Although made from 80% Grenache, it reminds me more of a Syrah; great wine either way..

112 Iroulèguy Tradition 2015, Domaine Arretxea France
12% **€29.50** Organic

Irouléguy Tradition 2015, Domaine Arretxea

TASTING NOTE
Vivid blackcurrant fruits, medium to full-bodied with good mineral notes and slightly austere tannins on the finish.

DRINK WITH
Eat as the locals would. Rare breast of duck with frites.

STYLE
Rounded & Fruity Red Wines

GRAPE VARIETY
66% Tannat, 17% Cabernet Franc, 17% Cabernet Sauvignon

BACKSTORY
Irouléguy is situated in the foothills of the Pyrenees, deep in south-west France, part of the Basque country. It makes its own unique wines. In the past they could be fairly austere and tannic; but wines such as this one are very approachable.

RICH AND FULL-BODIED RED WINES

113 **Merinas Old Vine Tempranillo 2018, Bodegas Fontana, Uclés**
Spain 14% **€10.50**
Organic, Vegan

STOCKISTS: Marks & Spencer, Marksandspencer.com

Merinas Old Vine Tempranillo 2018, Bodegas Fontana, Uclés

TASTING NOTE
A medium to full-bodied wine packed with supple, pure red-cherry fruits and a tannin-free rounded finish. Amazing value for money.

DRINK WITH
Drink it with grilled or barbecued white or red meats. Lamb chops with roasted lightly spicy red peppers and aubergines would be a fantastic match.

STYLE
Rich & Full-Bodied Red Wines

GRAPE VARIETY
Tempranillo

BACKSTORY
Uclés is part of La Mancha, the vast central plain of Spain. It is noted for producing high-quality Tempranillo, known here as Cencibel. These are often made in an easy-drinking fruity style, such as the one above. They are amongst my favourite 'glugging' wines

114 **Canfo Tempranillo 2017, Castilla-La Mancha, Bodegas Campos Reales**
Spain 13% **€13**

STOCKISTS: Listons, Dublin
2, listonsfoodstore.ie; Fallon &
Byrne, Dublin 2, fallonandbyrne.com; Clontarf Wines, Dublin 3
clontarfwines.ie; Ely 64, Glasthule, Ely64.com.

Canfo Tempranillo 2017, Castilla-La Mancha, Bodegas Campos Reales

TASTING NOTE
Medium-bodied and full of juicy ripe red fruits with soft tannins on the finish. A joyful glass of wine.

DRINK WITH
Perfect everyday wine to drink alongside most red and white meats, firm cheeses and most vegetarian dishes too.

STYLE
Rich & Full-Bodied Red Wines

GRAPE VARIETY
Tempranillo

BACKSTORY
The vast region of Castilla-La Mancha produces huge quantities of wine that can offer excellent value for money. Bodegas Campo Reales make a series of deliciously fruity, warming wines at great prices. This one is a steal.

115

**Passo Sardo 2016,
Cannonau di Sardegna**
Italy 14% **€14**

STOCKISTS: Jus de Vine, Portmarnock, jusdevine.ie; Ely 64, Glasthule, Ely64.com; Green Man Wines, Dublin 6, greenmanwines.ie; Clontarf Wines, Dublin 3 clontarfwines.ie; Kellys, Dublin 3, kellysofflicence. ie; McHughs, Dublin 5, mchughs. ie; Sweeneys D3, sweeneysd3.ie; Shiels, Malahide; MacGuinness Wines, Dundalk, dundalkwines. com; Fine Wines, Limerick; Joyce's Supermarket, Joycesupermarket.ie; Bradleys Off-licence, Cork, bradleysofflicence.ie.

Passo Sardo 2016, Cannonau di Sardegna

TASTING NOTE
Ripe strawberry fruits layered with warm spices.
Rounded and soft, this will come into its own as the
winter nights come in.

DRINK WITH
A good winter warmer, a casserole would be a perfect
partner.

STYLE
Rich & Full-Bodied Red Wines

GRAPE VARIETY
Cannonau/Carignan

BACKSTORY
Cannonau is what Grenache/Garnacha is called in Sardinia.
It was brought to the island centuries ago by the Spanish
and it makes delicious spicy rounded wines.

116 Petit Saó 2015, Costers del Segre
Spain 14.5% **€15.95**
Organic, Vegan

STOCKISTS: O'Briens, obrienswine.ie

Petit Saó 2015, Costers del Segre

TASTING NOTE
Ripe, sweet, leathery nose with masses of ripe dark fruits, good acidity and a solid tannic backbone. Needs food and an inquisitive palate.

DRINK WITH
A rich game pie or beef casserole.

STYLE
Rich & Full-Bodied Red Wines

GRAPE VARIETY
50% Tempranillo, 30% Garnacha, 20% Cabernet Sauvignon

BACKSTORY
Made from grapes grown on a 700h metre plateau in the Catalan D.O. of Costers del Segre, this is a wine that combines power with an enticing freshness.

117

Côtes du Rhône Saint-Esprit 2017, Delas
France 14% **€16.99**

STOCKISTS: The Corkscrew, Dublin 2, thecorkscrew.ie; Donnybrook Fair, donnybrookfair.ie; Coolers, Swords; Grapevine, Dalkey, onthegrapevine.ie; Higgins, Clonskeagh, Higginsfflicence.ie; O'Neills, D8; Nolans, D3, Nolans.ie; Kellys, Dublin 3, kellysofflicence.ie; The Malt House, Trim; 1601 Off-licence, Kinsale; Bradleys Off-licence, Cork, bradleysofflicence.ie; Ennis Gourmet Store, Ennis, ennisgourmet.com; Mortons of Galway, Mortonsofgalway.ie; Riney's, Sneem; The Grape & Grain, Co. Dublin, Leopardstowninn.ie; Shiel's, Malahide; Molloy's Liquor Stores, molloys.ie.

Côtes du Rhône Saint-Esprit 2017, Delas

TASTING NOTE
A rich, rounded, svelte Côtes du Rhône with smooth dark fruits and just the right amount of warmth.

DRINK WITH
Great with most meats; think barbecued red meats. A rare grilled steak, followed by some Comté.

STYLE
Rich & Full-Bodied Red Wines

250

GRAPE VARIETY
Syrah, Grenache.

BACKSTORY
The Southern Rhône valley produces massive quantities of decent glugging wine. Every supermarket offers one or more, usually at less than €10 and most of them are very drinkable. Spend a few euros more and you will find some great wines.

118

Jarrarte 2018 Rioja Joven, Abel Mendoza
Spain 13.5% €17

STOCKISTS: Cabot and Co., Westport, Cabotandco.com; Grapevine, Dalkey, onthegrapevine.ie; Market 57, Westport.

Jarrarte 2018 Rioja Joven, Abel Mendoza

TASTING NOTE
A full-on, full-bodied wine bursting with rounded sweet dark plum fruits and a tannin-free finish.

DRINK WITH
With a rack of lamb, as is traditional locally.

STYLE
Rich & Full-Bodied Red Wines

GRAPE VARIETY
Tempranillo

BACKSTORY
A glorious unoaked Rioja from husband and wife team Abel Mendoza and Maite Fernández, who make some of the most sought-after wines in the region.

119

**Carmen Gran Reserva
Cabernet Sauvignon
2017, Maipo**
Chile 13.5% **€18.50**

STOCKISTS: SuperValu, Supervalu.ie

Carmen Gran Reserva Cabernet Sauvignon 2017, Maipo

TASTING NOTE
Rich and smooth, with classic Cabernet red fruits and blackcurrants, subtle spicy oak, and a very long lingering dry finish. Impressive wine.

DRINK WITH
A spice-scented rack of lamb would do nicely.

STYLE
Rich and Full-bodied Red Wines

GRAPE VARIETY
Cabernet Sauvignon

BACKSTORY
The Maipo Valley is home to some of Chile's greatest Cabernet Sauvignon. This is a classic example, with some of the elegance of Bordeaux mixed in with the lush ripeness of California.

120

**Ruminat Primitivo
2018, IGT Terre di
Chieti** Italy 14% **€18.95**
Biodynamic, Vegan

STOCKISTS: O'Briens, obrienswine.ie

Ruminat Primitivo 2018, IGT Terre di Chieti

TASTING NOTE
Aromas of coffee, dark chocolate and loganberries; big, ripe, jammy sweet fruit with an earthy touch; powerful yet soft, it really delivers a mouthful of fruit.

DRINK WITH
With robust red meat dishes; spicy barbecued beef.

STYLE
Rich & Full-Bodied Red Wines

GRAPE VARIETY
Primitivo

BACKSTORY
Terre di Chieti is in the Abruzzo, best known for Montepulciano d'Abruzzo. But I really enjoyed this full-on Primitivo (otherwise known as Zinfandel) at a recent tasting.

121

D.O.C. Malbec 2016, Norton, Luján de Cuyo, Mendoza
Argentina 14%
€18.95/€12.95*

STOCKISTS: O'Briens, obrienswine.ie
*Price when on promotion

D.O.C. Malbec 2016, Norton, Luján de Cuyo, Mendoza

TASTING NOTE
A very well-made modern Malbec with clean pure loganberries and dark forest fruits, plus a light spiciness. Plenty of oomph but never over-powering.

DRINK WITH
The classic match would be a steak, but this would also partner a rack of lamb, or a loin of pork very nicely.

STYLE
Rich & Full-bodied Red Wines

GRAPE VARIETY
Malbec

BACKSTORY
Norton is owned by the Swarovski family (of jewellery fame). This Malbec is from the Luján de Cuyo D.O., home to some of the oldest vines in Argentina.

122

Dédicace 2017, Lirac, Domaine Coudoulis
France 15%
€19.95/€16.95* Vegan

STOCKISTS: O'Briens, obrienswine.ie
*Price when on promotion

Dédicace 2017, Lirac, Domaine Coudoulis

TASTING NOTE
This is a very good uncompromising Lirac; smooth, powerful and mouth-filling with masses of ripe slightly baked red cherries and dark fruits.

DRINK WITH
Drink with substantial dishes - roast or barbecued red meats, or winter casseroles.

STYLE
Rich & Full-bodied Red Wines

GRAPE VARIETY
Cinsault, Grenache, Syrah

BACKSTORY
Lirac lies just across the river from Châteauneuf-du-Pape in the Rhône Valley, and was once as well-known. Apart from the full-bodied but very approachable red wines, Lirac also produces impressive white wines and rosé.

123 Mimetic 2018, Gallinas de Piel, Calatayud
Spain 14.5% **€19.99** Vegan

STOCKISTS: Baggot Street Wines, Dublin 4, baggotstreetwines.com; Blackrock Cellar, Co Dublin, blackrockcellar.com; Bradley's, Cork, bradleysofflicence. ie; Cinnamon Cottage, cinnamoncottage.ie; Ely Wine Store, Co Kildare, elywinebar. ie; Jus de Vine, Portmarnock, Co Dublin, jusdevine.ie; Martins Off-Licence, Dublin 3, martinsofflicence.ie; Redmonds of Ranelagh, redmonds.ie; Stationtostationwine.ie

Mimetic 2018, Gallinas de Piel, Calatayud

TASTING NOTE
A rich and powerful wine with masses of smooth, ripe, dark fruits, offset perfectly by a subtle acidity and light tannins; gentle yet concentrated, this is an accomplished wine.

DRINK WITH
Grilled or barbecued red meats; a lightly smoky brisket?

STYLE
Rich & Full-bodied Red Wines

GRAPE VARIETY
Garnacha

BACKSTORY
Gallina de Piel is a project set up by David Seijas, formerly head sommelier at the famous El Bulli restaurant, and a former colleague, Ferran Centelles. The aim is to create a series of wines from the north of Spain, using indigenous grapes sourced from the finest vineyards, in this case the Calatayud region, famed for its Garnacha.

124 Garzón Tannat Reserva 2017
Uruguay 13.5% €20

263

STOCKISTS: Higgins, Clonskeagh, Higginsfflicence.ie; Drinkstore, D7, drinkstore.ie; MacGuinness Wines, Dundalk, dundalkwines.com; The Wine House, Trim; Deveneys, D14; Whelehan's Wines, Loughlinstown, whelehanswines.ie; Baggot Street Wines, Dublin 4, baggotstreetwines.com; Blackrock Cellar, Blackrock, blackrockcellar.com; D-Six Wines, Dublin 6; peggykellys.ie; Red Nose Wines, Clonmel, rednosewine.com; 1601 Off-licence, Kinsale; Gibney's, Malahide, gibneys.com; Kellys, Dublin 3, kellysofflicence.ie; The Parting Glass, Enniskerry; McHughs, Dublin 5, mchughs.ie; Ely Wine Store, Maynooth; elywinebar.ie; Clontarf Wines, Dublin 3 clontarfwines.ie; Swans on the Green, Naas.

Garzón Tannat Reserva 2017

TASTING NOTE
An intense and powerful wine with layers of brooding dark fruits, dark chocolate and spice. Structured and long.

DRINK WITH
Perfect with roast lamb.

STYLE
Rich & Full-bodied Red Wines

GRAPE VARIETY
Tannat

BACKSTORY
Basque immigrants from south-west France introduced Tannat, now the country's main grape variety, to Uruguay in the late 19th century. In its home territory of Madiran, Tannat can be fairly tannic, but in Uruguay it tends to be riper, softer and rounder.

125 Château Beauchêne Premier Terroir 2016, Côtes du Rhône
France 13.5% €20

STOCKISTS: 6Whelehan's Wines, Loughlinstown, whelehanswines.ie.

Château Beauchêne Premier Terroir 2016, Côtes du Rhône

TASTING NOTE
A very gluggable warming wine with lots of plump, ripe, dark fruits, and a seamless finish.

DRINK WITH
Something substantial; full-bodied autumn or winter casseroles.

STYLE
Rich & Full-bodied Red Wines

GRAPE VARIETY
70% Grenache 25% Syrah 5% Mourvèdre

BACKSTORY
This estate has been owned by the Bernard Family since 1794; part of it lies in Châteauneuf-du-Pape, and this wine bears a certain resemblance, at a much cheaper price.

126 Langhe Nebbiolo 2016, Pian delle Mole, Giulia Negri
Italy 13.5% **€27** Organic (in conversion) and Vegan

STOCKISTS: First Draft Coffee & Wine, Dublin 8, Firstdraftcoffeeandwine.com

Langhe Nebbiolo 2016, Pian delle Mole, Giulia Negri

TASTING NOTE
A very approachable Nebbiolo, without those bully-boy tannins; fragrant, elegant, piquant damsons and red cherries; medium-bodied with enticing pure fruit.

DRINK WITH
Feathered game, goose, steak or beef braised in Nebbiolo.

STYLE
Rich & Full-bodied Red Wines

GRAPE VARIETY
Nebbiolo

BACKSTORY
Giulia Negri, otherwise known as Barologirl, took over this estate in La Morra in Barolo at the age of 24. Undaunted by the task, she now not only produces three Barolos, but also this Nebbiolo, a Chardonnay and a Pinot Noir, the result of a trip to Burgundy. Sadly, only one of her Barolas and this Nebbiolo are currently available in Ireland.

127

Rioja Reserva 2012, La Granja Nuestra Senora de Remelluri, Remelluri Spain
14% **€32** Organic

STOCKISTS: Jus de Vine, Portmarnock, jusdevine.ie; Blackrock Cellar, Blackrock, blackrockcellar.com; Baggot Street Wines, Dublin 4, baggotstreetwines.com; Ely 64, Glasthule, Ely64.com; Clontarf Wines, Dublin 3 clontarfwines.ie; Green Man Wines, Dublin 6, greenmanwines.ie; Redmonds, Dublin 6; Redmonds.ie; Martins Off Licence, Dublin 3, martinsofflicence.ie; The Corkscrew, Dublin 2, thecorkscrew.ie; Whelehan's Wines, Loughlinstown, whelehanswines.ie; The Wine Centre, Kilkenny, Thewinecentre.ie.

Rioja Reserva 2012, La Granja Nuestra Senora de Remelluri, Remelluri

TASTING NOTE
Supremely elegant with pointed pure dark cherry and blackcurrant fruits; there is a hint of spice, excellent structure and grip, with a lingering long dry finish.

DRINK WITH
With a roast leg of lamb.

STYLE
Rich & Full-bodied Red Wines

GRAPE VARIETY
Tempranillo, Garnacha, Graciano

BACKSTORY
Telmo Rodriguez is one of the greatest winemakers in Spain; over the last two decades he has led the drive to rediscover forgotten regions and grape varieties around the country. Now he has returned to his native Rioja to produce terroir-driven wines in a region noted for blending across the entire area.

128

Selección de Bodega Malbec 2016, Doña Paula, Alluvia Vineyard, Gualtallary
Artgentina 13.5% **€35**

STOCKISTS: Deveney's, D14;
Jus de Vine, Portmarnock, jusdevine.ie; Redmonds, Dublin 6;
Redmonds.ie.

Selección de Bodega Malbec 2016, Doña Paula, Alluvia Vineyard, Gualtallary

TASTING NOTE
A powerful full-bodied wine, loaded with concentrated, fresh, cool, dark fruits, underpinned by a firm mineral core, finishing with some real grip and tannins. A very impressive wine.

DRINK WITH
Steak would be traditional, but any red meat would do nicely here.

STYLE
Rich & Full-bodied Red Wines

GRAPE VARIETY
Malbec

BACKSTORY
The Selección de Bodega comes from the high-altitude Alluvia vineyard in Gualtallary, Uco Valley. This sub-region contains a mix of limestone and alluvial soils, and is fast becoming the most sought-after part of the Uco Valley.

129

Gianni Brunelli Rosso di Montalcino 2017
Italy 13.5% €38

273

Gianni Brunelli Rosso di Montalcino 2017

TASTING NOTE
Beautifully fragrant – all violets and strawberries; very forward with elegant, concentrated, ripe red cherry fruit, and a fine line of savoury tannin. Delicious wine.

DRINK WITH
A roast of beef or lamb, a bistecca alla fiorentina, or a firm cheese - aged Pecorino sounds good.

STYLE
Rich and Full-bodied Reds

GRAPE VARIETY
Sangiovese

BACKSTORY
A tasting of various vintages of Gianni Brunelli's Brunello di Montalcino earlier this year was fantastic; sadly they are not cheap. However, this Rosso di Montalcino was excellent, (relatively) less expensive and ready to drink now.

130

Anthill Farms 2016 Syrah, Campbell Ranch Vineyard, Sonoma Coast USA
13.8% **€40**
Biodynamic, Vegan

ANTHILL FARMS 2016 SYRAH
Sonoma Coast
Campbell Ranch Vineyard

STOCKISTS: Mitchell & Son,
Dublin 1, Sandycove, and
Avoca, Kilmacanogue & Dunboyne, mitchellandson.com; Ely
Wine Store, Maynooth; elywinebar.ie.

Anthill Farms 2016 Syrah, Campbell Ranch Vineyard, Sonoma Coast

TASTING NOTE
Ripe, rounded, dark berries and subtle spice; a beguiling and very seductive mix of elegance and power.

DRINK WITH
Roast pheasant or venison.

STYLE
Rich and Full-bodied Reds

GRAPE VARIETY
Syrah

BACKSTORY
Webster Marquez, Anthony Filiberti and David Low met while working at gourmet store Sonoma Williams; they farm and make wine (mainly Pinot Noir) from vineyards along the cool Sonoma Coast region in Northern California.

NATURAL WINE

131 Custoza Boscroi 2018, Monte dei Roari Italy 12% €17 Biodynamic

279

STOCKISTS: Sheridan's Cheesemongers, South Anne Street, Kells, Co. Meath, Galway, sheridanscheesemongers. com; SIYPS.com; Ely 64, Glasthule, Ely64.com.

Custoza Boscroi 2018, Monte dei Roari

TASTING NOTE
Delicate floral aromas, rich and long texture with almonds, orange peel and a lively acidity.

DRINK WITH
Grilled white fish with a squeeze of lemon.

STYLE
Natural

GRAPE VARIETY
Trebbiano di Soave, Garganega, Fernanda, Trebbianello

BACKSTORY
Fermented and aged in amphorae and then bottled without fining or filtering; it all makes for an intriguing and delicious glass of wine.

132

Bardolino "Reboi" 2018, Monte dei Roari
Italy 12.5% €17
Biodynamic

281

STOCKISTS: Sheridan's Cheesemongers, South Anne Street, Kells, Co. Meath, Galway, sheridanscheesemongers.com; SIYPS.com; Green Man Wines, Terenure, greenmanwines.ie; Blackrock Cellar, Blackrock, blackrockcellar.com; Ely 64, Glasthule, Ely64.com

Bardolino "Reboi" 2018, Monte dei Roari

TASTING NOTE
Very inviting juicy, piquant, black cherries and plums; fresh and very easy to drink.

DRINK WITH
With some salumi, mild cheeses and good crusty sour-dough bread.

STYLE
Natural

GRAPE VARIETY
Corvina, Corvinone, Rondinella, Molinara and Rossignola

BACKSTORY
This is a small biodynamically-farmed family estate. The Reboi is made using local yeasts, in a concrete egg, with a minimal addition of sulphur. It all works very well.

133 Ink 2018, Judith Beck, Burgenland
Austria 12.5% **€17.95**
Biodynamic/Natural

STOCKISTS: Baggot Street Wines; Blackrock Cellars; Loose Canon; Le Caveau; Bradleys Off License Cork; Cass & Co Dungarvan; Clontarf Wines; Fallon and Byrne; The Drink Store Stneybatter; Green Man Wines; The Corkscrew; Redmonds Ranelagh; Martins Off License; 64 Wines

Ink 2018, Judith Beck, Burgenland

TASTING NOTE
Crunchy, vibrant black cherry and damson fruits with a lively, refreshing acidity.

DRINK WITH
Serve very lightly chilled with grilled chicken or pork.

STYLE
Natural

GRAPE VARIETY
70% Zweigelt, 30% St. Laurent

BACKSTORY
Having gained wine-making experience around the world, Judith Beck joined the family estate in 2001, taking full control in 2004. About 85% of the vineyards are red, including three native Austrian varieties, Blaufränkisch, Zweigelt and St. Laurent.

134

**Vola Vole 2018,
Trebbiano d'Abruzzo**
Italy 12.5% **€17.95/13.95***
Organic, Vegan,
Certified Bee-friendly

285

Vola Vole 2018, Trebbiano d'Abruzzo

TASTING NOTE
Lightly textured with yellow apples, autumn fruits, a honeyed touch and a crisp dry finish.

DRINK WITH
A margherita pizza or seafood risotto.

STYLE
Natural

GRAPE VARIETY
Trebbiano

BACKSTORY
Trebbiano is not generally noted for producing interesting wines, but this is an exception. Certified bee friendly - they protect the habitat - the fermentation yeasts are selected from pollen the bees collect in the surrounding wildlife parks.

135

**Pheasant's Tears
Saperavi 2018**
Georgia 13% **€23.95**
Organic/Natural

STOCKISTS: Bradleys Off
License; The Corkscrew; Redmonds Ranelagh; Le Caveau
Kilkenny; Green Man Wines

Pheasant's Tears Saperavi 2018

TASTING NOTE
A quite unique wine, dark and earthy, with musky spices, tar and all sorts of deep, unfathomable flavours, finishing with firm dry tannins.

DRINK WITH
Food would certainly be good; chakapuli - traditional Georgian lamb stew.

STYLE
Natural

GRAPE VARIETY
Saperavi

BACKSTORY
I had a memorable tasting with John Wurdeman of Pheasant's Tears (in Ireland sadly) earlier this year. He is one of the driving forces behind the revival of interest in Georgian wines. We went through 12 fascinating, completely unique wines, all made from ancient Georgian varieties.

136

Rivera del Notro
2017, Itata, Roberto Henríques
Chile 12% €24
Biodynamic

STOCKISTS: Loose Canon, 29 Drury St., loosecanon.ie; Green Man Wines, Terenure, greenmanwines.ie; Blackrock Cellar, Blackrock, blackrockcellar.com; The Coach House, Ballinteer, thecoachhouseofflicence.ie.

Rivera del Notro 2017, Itata, Roberto Henríques

TASTING NOTE
A very engaging, gently perfumed 'vin de soif' or thirst quencher,that mixes nicely textured plump orange and pear fruits, with a reviving mineral acidity and a long dry finish.

DRINK WITH
By itself or with grilled sea bass/bream.

STYLE
Natural

GRAPE VARIETY
Semillón, Moscatel, Corinto

BACKSTORY
Roberto Henríquez is a mild-mannered intelligent man who is quietly making a name for himself. From the south of Chile, he travelled the world having completed his winemaking studies. On returning home, he began making very low-intervention wines from ancient vineyards. This skin contact wine is made using natural yeasts, and tiny amounts of sulphur.

137

Verdicchio dei Castelli di Jeso Classico Superiore Capovolto 2018, La Marca di San Michele Italy 13%
€24 Biodynamic

291

STOCKISTS: Sheridan's Cheesemongers, South Anne Street, Kells, Co. Meath, Galway, sheridanscheesemongers.com; SIYPS.com; Ely 64, Glasthule, Ely64.com.

Verdicchio dei Castelli di Jeso Classico Superiore Capovolto 2018, La Marca di San Michele

TASTING NOTE
A fascinating and seductive wine with rich, textured, citrus peel, lush peach fruits, almonds and a rounded finish.

DRINK WITH
Pasta with seafood and lemon.

STYLE
Natural

GRAPE VARIETY
Verdicchio

BACKSTORY
Last year I featured the Saltatempo from this producer; this year, the Capovolto, aged for 6-9 months on its lees. Both are remarkable wines.

138 Unlitro 2018, Ampelia
IGT Costa Toscana
Italy 12% **€24.50**
Organic/Natural

STOCKISTS: Baggot Street
Wines; Blackrock Cellars; Loose Canon; Le Caveau; Bradleys
Off License Cork; Cass & Co Dungarvan; Green Man Wines;
Redmonds Ranelagh; Ely 64, Glasthule, Ely64.com.

Unlitro 2018, Ampelia IGT Costa Toscana

TASTING NOTE
A wonderful mix of fresh smooth summer fruits -
cherries, strawberries, redcurrants, - and wild herbs.

DRINK WITH
Comfortable with a wide range of foods, including
mixed mezze, roast Mediterranean vegetables, grilled
lamb with tahini.

STYLE
Natural

GRAPE VARIETY
Grenache, Carignan and Alicante Bouschet

BACKSTORY
This also featured last year; it is one of those great all-
purpose wines, made by Elisabetta Foradori, one of the
leading natural winemakers of Italy.

139

Benje Tinto, Envínate, Ycoden-Daute-Isora, Tenerife 2017
Spain 12.5% **€28**
Organic not certified.
Vegan Friendly

STOCKISTS: Green Man Wines, Dublin 6, greenmanwines.ie; Deveney's D14.

Benje Tinto, Envínate, Ycoden-Daute-Isora, Tenerife 2017

TASTING NOTE
Very light in colour and body; red cherries and plums with an earthy edge, a mineral backbone and a tannin-free finish. Gorgeous wine.

DRINK WITH
On its own, lightly chilled, or with mixed tapas.

STYLE
Natural

GRAPE VARIETY
Listan Prieto

BACKSTORY
Fancy something different? Most of the wines from the Canary Islands are made from unique local grapes and often from ungrafted vines. I feature two in *WoW 2020*, both made by very low intervention methods. The results are amazing.

FINE WINES

140

**Sandhi Pinot Noir
2017, Sta. Rita Hills,
California**
USA 13% **€38** Organic

STOCKISTS: Grapevine,
Dalkey, onthegrapevine.ie;
stationtostationwine.com; Deveney's, D14; Blackrock Cellar,
Blackrock, blackrockcellar.com.

Sandhi Pinot Noir 2017, Sta. Rita Hills, California

TASTING NOTE
Fragrant and intense with plenty of sweet/sour dark cherry fruits, hints of spice, and real depth. Smooth, elegant and aristocratic Pinot Noir.

DRINK WITH
Roast wild duck or other feathered game.

STYLE
Fine Wine

GRAPE VARIETY
Pinot Noir

BACKSTORY
Rajat Parr and Sashi Moorman, who run Sandhi and Domaine de la Côte in California and Evening Land in Oregon, make some of the most exciting and sought-after Chardonnay and Pinot Noir. Indian-American Parr is a former top sommelier while California-born Moorman is of Japanese/American ethnicity. Together they make a number of awesome American wines, some of which have previously featured in this guide.

141

Chablis 1er cru Vaulorent 2015, La Chablisienne
France 13.5% **€40**

STOCKISTS: Jus de Vine, Portmarnock, jusdevine. ie; Redmonds, Ranelagh; Redmonds.ie; The Vintry, Dublin 6, vintry.ie; Cashel Wine Cellar, cashel.ie; Sweeney's D3, sweeneysd3.ie; Swans on the Green, Naas; Baggot Street Wines, Dublin 4, baggotstreetwines.com; J.J. O'Driscoll, Ballinlough, jjodriscoll.ie; 1601 Off-licence, Kinsale; McHughs, Dublin 5, mchughs.ie; Deveney's, D14; Thomas's of Foxrock, thomasoffoxrock.ie.

Chablis 1er cru Vaulorent 2015, La Chablisienne

TASTING NOTE
Alluring, sophisticated, exotic fruits given shape by a backbone of fine cool minerality; it finishes dry, showing great persistence. Excellent, exciting wine.

DRINK WITH
Boiled lobster with something buttery or grilled black sole with buerre blanc.

STYLE
Fine Wine

GRAPE VARIETY
Chardonnay

BACKSTORY
La Chablisienne is one of the best co-ops in France, with a treasure-trove of wines from most of the Premier and Grand Cru sites of Chablis. The winemaking is exemplary.

142

**Bodega Colomé'
Auténtico' Salta Malbec
2017** Argentina 14.5%
€41.99 Biodynamic

STOCKISTS: Wineonline.ie;
The Cinnamon Cottage, Cork,
cinnamoncottage.ie; The Corkscrew, Chatham St.,
thecorkscrew.ie: Donnybrook Fair, donnybrookfair.ie.

Bodega Colomé 'Auténtico' Salta Malbec 2017

TASTING NOTE
Enchanting aromas of violets and dark fruits. The wine explodes in the mouth with intense perfectly ripe dark fruits, balanced by excellent acidity and structured tannins.

DRINK WITH
Keep a few years or serve now with grilled beef or lamb.

STYLE
Fine Wines

GRAPE VARIETY
Malbec

BACKSTORY
Bodegas Colomé is the oldest functioning winery in Argentina, having been founded in 1831. A bumpy two-hour drive from civilisation, it is home to some of the oldest and highest vineyards in the world, with vines growing at 1,750-3,100 metres above sea level.

143

Etna Rosso Guardiola 2017, Tenuta delle Terre Nere Italy 14.5%
€45 Organic, Vegan

STOCKISTS: Blackrock Cellar, Blackrock, blackrockcellar.com

Etna Rosso Guardiola 2017, Tenuta delle Terre Nere

TASTING NOTE
Elegant, high-toned, cool, savoury red fruits – redcurrants and cherries - with a taut structure, and fine drying tannins and minerals on the finish. Fantastic concentration and depth. Magnificent wine.

DRINK WITH
Keep for a year or two, or, if you must open it now, decant and drink alongside roast or grilled pork with tomato-based sauce of some kind.

STYLE
Fine Wines

GRAPE VARIETY
Nerello Mascalese and Nerello Cappuccio

BACKSTORY
Thirty years ago, Marco de Grazia, an American wine importer, was among the first to set up an estate on the northern slopes of Mount Etna. This is from a single vineyard, one of the highest plots at around 1,000 metres. Di Grazia describes it as "an austere taut coiled spring", and "a soprano of a wine".

144

Viña Tondonia 2006, Bodegas López de Heredia, Rioja Reserva Blanco Spain 12.5% €45

STOCKISTS: Jus de Vine, Portmarnock, jusdevine. ie; La Touche, Greystones, Latouchewines4u.ie; Ely 64, Glasthule, Ely64.com; Baggot Street Wines, Dublin 4, baggotstreetwines.com; Blackrock Cellar, Blackrock, blackrockcellar. com; Green Man Wines, Dublin 6, greenmanwines.ie; Clontarf Wines, Dublin 3 clontarfwines. ie; Redmonds, Dublin 6; Redmonds.ie; Whelehan's Wines, Loughlinstown, whelehanswines. ie; The Corkscrew, Dublin 2, thecorkscrew.ie; SIYPS.com; Sweeney's D3, sweeneysd3.ie; Martin's Off Licence, Dublin 3, martinsofflicence.ie.

Viña Tondonia 2006, Bodegas López de Heredia, Rioja Reserva Blanco

TASTING NOTE
A glorious mix of dried fruit, toasted nuts, and orange peel with a funky, slightly earthy, oxidative note. A marmite wine to be sure, but then I love marmite.

DRINK WITH
The website recommends all kinds of grilled fish, seafood risotto, or chicken, turkey, duck or rabbit!

STYLE
Fine Wines

GRAPE VARIETY
Viura, Malvasia

BACKSTORY
López de Heredia is one of the legendary old-style producers in Rioja; they age wines for long periods, sometimes decades in both cask and bottle, before release. The wines are unique, individual and full of character.

145

Pavillon de Léoville Poyferré 2015, St. Julien France 13.5% €45

STOCKISTS: Whelehan's Wines, Loughlinstown, whelehanswines.ie

Pavillon de Léoville Poyferré 2015, St. Julien

TASTING NOTE
A classic Saint Julien nose of lead pencils and perfectly ripe blackcurrant fruits; the palate is elegant but concentrated with plump fruits, fine tannins, and a lovely long dry finish; a very impressive wine.

DRINK WITH
A roast of lamb with rosemary and garlic.

STYLE
Fine Wines

GRAPE VARIETY
61% Cabernet Sauvignon, 27% Merlot, 8% Petit Verdot, 4% Cabernet Franc

BACKSTORY
This is the second wine of Ch Léoville-Poyferré, one of the three great Léoville Chateaux of Saint-Julien. In Bordeaux terms, it is very good value for money.

146

**As Sortes 2017,
Rafael Palacios,
Valdeorras**
Spain 14% **€46**
Biodynamic

STOCKISTS: Ely 64,
Glasthule, Ely64.com;
Baggot Street Wines, Dublin
4, baggotstreetwines.
com; Blackrock Cellar,
Blackrock, blackrockcellar.
com; Clontarf Wines,
Dublin 3 clontarfwines.
ie; SIYPS.com; Whelehan's
Wines, Loughlinstown,
whelehanswines.ie;
The Corkscrew, Dublin
2, thecorkscrew.ie; La
Touche, Greystones,
Latouchewines4u.ie; Sweeney's D3, sweeneysd3.ie; Green
Man Wines, Dublin 6, greenmanwines.ie.

As Sortes 2017, Rafael Palacios, Valdeorras

TASTING NOTE
A medium-bodied wine with texture, complexity and real depth. Ripe peach and apple fruits, subtle toasted hazelnuts, all kept in perfect harmony by a crisp saline mineral streak.

DRINK WITH
Richer fish dishes such as grilled turbot or black sole. Alternatively a herb and lemon stuffed roast chicken.

STYLE
Fine Wines

GRAPE VARIETY
Godello

BACKSTORY
Not cheap, but Rafael Palacios makes some of the finest dry white wines in Spain. If you are a fan of white Burgundy, this should be right up your street; one of my favourites.

147 Brunello di Montalcino 2014, Col d'Orcia
Italy 14.5% €48 Organic

STOCKISTS: Sheridan's Cheesemongers, Dublin 2, Kells, Co. Meath, Galway, sheridanscheesemongers.com; Green Man Wines, Dublin 6, greenmanwines.ie; Fallon & Byrne, Rathmines, fallonandbyrne. com; Ely 64, Glasthule, Ely64. com; Mitchell & Son, Dublin 1, Sandycove, and Avoca, Kilmacanogue & Dunboyne, mitchellandson.com.

Brunello di Montalcino 2014, Col d'Orcia

TASTING NOTE
Big, powerful, muscular wine crammed with pure dark fruits, structured tannins, and a smooth, long, long finish. Excellent now but will continue to evolve.

DRINK WITH
A grilled steak would be perfect or baked stuffed mushrooms.

STYLE
Fine Wines

GRAPE VARIETY
Sangiovese

BACKSTORY
Owned by Count Francesco Marone Cinzano since the early 1970s, this is one of the most highly rated producers of Montalcino, a region close to Chianti Classico that rose to fame largely in the 20th century. Brunello is one of the most long-lived wines of Italy.

148 2016 Chablis 1er Cru Mont de Milieu, Domaine Christophe
France 13% €49

315

STOCKISTS: SIYPS.com; Ely Wine Store, Maynooth; elywinebar.ie.

2016 Chablis 1er Cru Mont de Milieu, Domaine Christophe

TASTING NOTE

An enchanting complex floral nose; beautifully balanced ripe apple fruits with lime zest; elegant and restrained with a fine seam of mineral acidity. A classic Chablis of the highest order.

DRINK WITH

Oysters or even better gougères, those gorgeous cheesy choux pastry puffs would be great, but ideally, I would keep this for a main course; poached salmon with home-made mayonnaise, or grilled sole with masses of butter and herbs.

STYLE

Fine Wines

GRAPE VARIETY

Chardonnay

BACKSTORY

Clearly this is not cheap, but it was one of my favourite wines from a recent tasting of Chablis Premiers Crus and is certainly worth it. I would happily lay it down for a few years, but it is a pleasure to drink now. This is a small estate, started as recently as 1999.

149

Pretty Pony 2013, Kanaan Winery, Ningxia Helan Mountain China 14%
€49.99

STOCKISTS: The Corkscrew, Dublin 2, thecorkscrew.ie; Wineonline.ie; Mitchell & Son, Dublin 1, Sandycove, and Avoca, Kilmacanogue & Dunboyne, mitchellandson.com; Terroirs, Dublin 4, Terroirs.ie; The Wine House, Trim; Redmonds, Dublin 6; Redmonds.ie.

Pretty Pony 2013, Kanaan Winery, Ningxia Helan Mountain

TASTING NOTE
Made from 90% Cabernet Sauvignon, this has damsons, forest fruits and dark chocolate the on nose and palate, with fine dry tannins and good acidity.

DRINK WITH
Grilled or roast red meats

STYLE
Fine Wines

GRAPE VARIETY
90% Cabernet Sauvignon, 10% Merlot

BACKSTORY
Only Spain has more land under vines than China. This wine comes from Ningxia, known for cold winters where temperatures fall to -20°C; each vine has to be buried manually in November before being dug up the following April. This is the first Chinese wine included in the guide, but, trade wars allowing, I don't expect it to be the last.

150

Sandhi Sanford & Benedict Chardonnay 2016 USA 13.5% €50
Organic

SANFORD & BENEDICT
STA. RITA HILLS CHARDONNAY '16

Sandhi

STOCKISTS: Ely 64, Glasthule,
Ely64.com; stationtostationwine.
com; Redmonds, Dublin 6; Redmonds.ie; Blackrock Cellar,
Blackrock, blackrockcellar.com.

Sandhi Sanford & Benedict Chardonnay 2016

TASTING NOTE
White flower aromas, subtle fresh lemon and peach
fruits, interwoven with light oak; a wine of great
complexity and character.

DRINK WITH
Grilled black sole with maître d' butter.

STYLE
Fine Wines

GRAPE VARIETY
Chardonnay

BACKSTORY
One of the Sandhi Pinot Noirs also features in this guide. It is
great to see these wonderful wines available in some sort of
quantity in Ireland.

151

Two Paddocks 'The Fusilier' Pinot Noir 2017, Central Otago New Zealand
13% **€50** Biodynamic

STOCKISTS: Gibney's, Malahide, gibneys.com; Cashel Wine Cellar, Cashel, cashel.wine.cellar@hotmail.com; The Wine House, Trim.

Two Paddocks 'The Fusilier' Pinot Noir 2017, Central Otago

TASTING NOTE
Silky and smooth with a wonderful concentration of dark cherry fruits, hints of spice, nice grip and a long finish. Right out of the top drawer.

DRINK WITH
Try this with grilled garlicky lamb chops.

STYLE
Fine Wines

GRAPE VARIETY
Pinot Noir

BACKSTORY
Two Paddocks is owned by film star Sam Neill and 'The Fusilier' is a single vineyard on the Felton Road in Central Otago. It is named after Neill's father, Major Dermot Neill, who served in the Royal Irish Fusiliers. Sam Neill was born in Northern Ireland and the family later moved to New Zealand.

152 **Trefiano 2015,
Carmignano Riserva
2015, Capezzana** Italy
14.5% **€54.99**
Organic, Vegan

D.O.C.G.

Vittorio Contini Bonacossi

TREFIANO

RISERVA 2015

CARMIGNANO
D.O.C.G.

CAPEZZANA
CONTE CONTINI BONACOSSI

STOCKISTS: Ely Wine Store,
Maynooth, Co Kildare, Ely 64 Wine,Co Dublin, 64wine.
ie; Stationtostationwine.ie; Terroirs, Dublin 4, terroirs.ie;
Wineonline.ie

Trefiano 2015, Carmignano Riserva 2015, Capezzana

TASTING NOTE
A rich powerful wine with concentrated, herbal, ripe dark fruits, well-integrated tannins, and a lingering finish.

DRINK WITH
A full-bodied dish to match the wine: game dishes or a rib eye.

STYLE
Fine Wines

GRAPE VARIETY
80% Sangiovese, 10% Cabernet Sauvignon, 10% Canaiolo

BACKSTORY
Capezzana in Carmignano is one of the oldest vineyards in Tuscany dating from around 804 AD. It is owned by the Contini Bonacossi family and is a long-established organic producer. As well as making very good wines, the family produces an excellent olive oil, and also runs a cookery school in the beautiful property.

153

**Barolo Castiglione
2015, Vietti, Piemonte**
Italy 13.5% **€55** Vegan

325

STOCKISTS: Avoca,
Ballsbridge & Rathcoole, Avoca.
com; Mitchell & Son, Dublin 1, Sandycove, and Avoca,
Kilmacanogue & Dunboyne, mitchellandson.com.

Barolo Castiglione 2015, Vietti, Piemonte

TASTING NOTE
A very fine elegant wine with enticing violet aromas, clean ripe dark fruits, some tobacco and good firm tannins on the finish. A wine with good structure; keep for five years.

DRINK WITH
With roast game, beef casseroles or mushroom risotto.

STYLE
Fine Wines

GRAPE VARIETY
Nebbiolo

BACKSTORY
One of the top Barolo houses; the 2013 featured last year. The 2015 is a worthy successor.

154

Tolpuddle Vineyard Pinot Noir 2017, Coal River, Tasmania
Australia 13% €62.99
Vegan

STOCKISTS: Avoca, avoca. com; Baggot Street Wines, Dublin 4, baggotstreetwines. com; Blackrock Cellar, Co Dublin, blackrockcellar.com; Ely Wine Store - Maynooth, Ely 64 Wine, Co Dublin 64wine.ie; Jus de Vine, Portmarnock, Co Dublin, jusdevine.ie; Mitchell & Son, Dublin 1, Sandycove, and Avoca, Kilmacanogue & Dunboyne, mitchellandson.com; Redmonds of Ranelagh, redmonds. ie; Stationtostationwine.ie; The Corkscrew, Chatham St, thecorkscrew.ie; Wineonline.ie.

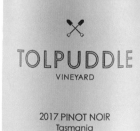

Tolpuddle Vineyard Pinot Noir 2017, Coal River, Tasmania

TASTING NOTE
Fragrant, refined and elegant with exquisite pure dark cherry fruits, hints of spice, and refreshing throughout. A huge level of concentration in a relatively light (13%) wine.

DRINK WITH
With duck in all its forms, roast chicken or pork.

STYLE
Fine Wine

GRAPE VARIETY
Pinot Noir

BACKSTORY
This is one of the most talked-about and sought-after wines of Australia. Cousins Martin Shaw and Michael Hill-Smith (of Hill-Smith fame in the Adelaide Hills) bought this vineyard in cool-climate Tasmania in 2011. Their first vintage was 2012, and each succeeding vintage has garnered huge critical acclaim. The vineyard, which was established in 1988, is called after the Tolpuddle Martyrs, English convicts transported to Tasmania for forming an agricultural union. The leader of the Martyrs, George Loveless, served some of his sentence working on a property near Richmond, part of which is now Tolpuddle Vineyard.

155

Corison Cabernet Sauvignon 2014, Napa Valley, California

USA 14% **€132** Organic

2 0 1 4

CORISON

ST. HELENA
NAPA VALLEY
CABERNET
SAUVIGNON

STOCKISTS: Green Man Wines, Dublin 6, greenmanwines.ie

Corison Cabernet Sauvignon 2014, Napa Valley, California

TASTING NOTE
Enchanting wine; ripe blackcurrant, cassis and dark cherries with herbs and an attractive earthiness underpinned by a fine tannic structure.

DRINK WITH
Ideally decant it before drinking alongside a plain rare roast of beef or lamb. The wine is the undoubted star here.

STYLE
Fine Wine

GRAPE VARIETY
Cabernet Sauvignon

BACKSTORY
Cathy Corison crafts some of greatest Cabernet Sauvignon of the Napa Valley. The wines are always impeccably balanced, full-bodied yet elegant, refined but full of wonderful Cab flavours. According to her website, the images on the Corison labels are inspired by old life symbols based on rain and a sprouting seed. 'They embellished vases excavated from the site of one of the earliest European cultures to cultivate grapes and make wine over 7,000 years ago.' And yes, it is a ridiculous sum of money for a single bottle of wine. But it is a ridiculously good wine.

FORTIFIED WINES

156

Marks & Spencer Manzanilla
Spain 15% **€12**

333

Marks & Spencer Manzanilla

TASTING NOTE
Light, fruity, tangy and fresh; a perfect aperitif sherry and an absolute steal for €12.

DRINK WITH
Fino and Manzanilla go amazingly well with just about any food, particularly anything deep-fried or salty. Perfect with mixed tapas.

STYLE
Fortified Wines

GRAPE VARIETY
Palomino Fino

BACKSTORY
I am a huge fan of all kinds of sherry but my favourite is possibly a well-chilled glass (or two) of Fino or Manzanilla served with a few nibbles.

157

Gabriela Pago Balbaina, Sanchez Ayala, Manzanilla Spain 15%
€12 per ½ bottle

STOCKISTS: Worldwide Wines, Waterford, worldwidewines.ie; Le Caveau, Kilkenny, lecaveau.ie.

Gabriela Pago Balbaina, Sanchez Ayala, Manzanilla

TASTING NOTE
This is quite lovely; fresh intense nose, lightly floral with a bready note; the palate has almonds, lovely subtle fruit, excellent length, and real character, finishing dry. A must-try.

DRINK WITH
All kinds of seafood, or sushi and sashimi.

STYLE
Fortified Wines

GRAPE VARIETY
Palomino Fino

BACKSTORY
This is one of the finest Manzanilla sherries of all. It is named after the 19th century singer and dancer Gabriela Ortega Feria. The company, bought in 1986 by businessman José-Luis Barrera, owns 90 hectares of vines. The Gabriela is a single-vineyard wine, from the Las Cañas vineyard in the Pago Balbaina. It is fermented with natural yeasts, aged for 5-6 years under flor in barrel, and very lightly filtered.

158

Callejuela Manzanilla Fina NV Spain 15% €18

STOCKISTS: Ely 64, Glasthule, Ely64.com; Baggot Street Wines, Dublin 4, baggotstreetwines. com; Blackrock Cellar, Blackrock, blackrockcellar.com; Green Man Wines, Dublin 6, greenmanwines. ie; The Corkscrew, Dublin 2, thecorkscrew.ie; Jus de Vine, Portmarnock, jusdevine.ie; Redmonds, Dublin 6; Redmonds.ie; Whelehan's Wines, Loughlinstown, whelehanswines.ie; The Wicklow Wine Co., Wicklow, wicklowwineco. ie; Martin's Off Licence, Dublin 3, martinsofflicence.ie; SIYPS.cor

Callejuela Manzanilla Fina NV

TASTING NOTE
Light and refreshing as a Manzanilla should be, with crisp biting acidity, and intense, bready, toasted almond flavours. Brilliant sherry. Their Manzanilla Pasada Blanquito is even better, but difficult to find.

DRINK WITH
A plate of mixed tapas would be perfect.

STYLE
Fortified Wines

GRAPE VARIETY
Palomino Fino

BACKSTORY
Callejuela was founded in 1980 by Francisco Blanco Martinez, a vineyard worker. He succeeded in slowly building up holdings in some of the finest vineyards all over the region. His two sons, Pepe and Paco, now run the winery, and have turned it into one of the very best producers in the region, focusing on single-vineyard wines.

159
Oloroso, Marqués de Poley, Montilla-Moriles, Toro Albalá
Spain 17% **€19.95**

STOCKISTS: O'Briens, obrienswine.ie

Oloroso, Marqués de Poley, Montilla-Moriles, Toro Albalá

TASTING NOTE
Rich amber in colour; rounded, with walnuts, old polished wood, fragrant spices and dried fruits, finishing dry. A fascinating glass of wine.

DRINK WITH
With chicken or beef consommé, or dishes featuring chorizo.

STYLE
Fortified Wines

GRAPE VARIETY
Pedro Ximénez

BACKSTORY
The Montilla-Moriles region lies close to Jerez, home of sherry, and has very similar customs and traditions. The wines cannot be called sherry as they lie outside the demarcated region. Using the Pedro Ximénez grape instead of the Palomino Fino of Jerez, the region produces some exquisite wines.

160

Taylor's Late-Bottled Vintage Port 2014
Portugal 20% €24

STOCKISTS: Jus de Vine, Portmarnock, jusdevine. ie; Clontarf Wines, Dublin 3 clontarfwines.ie; Green Man Wines, Dublin 6, greenmanwines. ie; Kellys, Dublin 3, kellysofflicence. ie; Gibney's, Malahide, gibneys. com; Terroirs, Dublin 4, Terroirs. ie; McHughs, Dublin 5, mchughs. ie; Mitchell & Son, Dublin 1, Sandycove, and Avoca, Kilmacanogue & Dunboyne, mitchellandson.com; Sweeneys D3, sweeneysd3.ie; Wineonline. ie; Le Caveau, Kilkenny, lecaveau.ie; O'Donovan's, Cork, Odonovansofflicence. com; MacGuinness Wines, Dundalk, dundalkwines.com; Fine Wines, Limerick; Joyce's Supermarket, Galway, Joycesupermarket.ie.

Taylor's Late-Bottled Vintage Port 2014

TASTING NOTE
Smooth warming red berry fruits and Christmas cake spice, with a soft rounded finish.

DRINK WITH

With blue cheese or dark chocolate desserts.

STYLE
Fortified Wines

GRAPE VARIETY
Touriga Nacional, Touriga Francesa, Tinto Cão, Tinta Roriz, Tinta Barroca

BACKSTORY
LBV, or late-bottled vintage port, is allowed to develop for several years in the cellar, making it far less tannic and more approachable than its big brother, vintage port.

161 El Maestro Sierra Fino
Spain 15% **€25.99**

343

El Maestro Sierra Fino

TASTING NOTE
Wow! This fairly explodes with flavour; full of character,
dry with classic almonds and green apples, savoury, with
an earthy touch too.

DRINK WITH
As with all fino, this should be served chilled with all
kinds of nibbles/tapas, or alternatively deep-fried fish.

STYLE
Fortified Wines

GRAPE VARIETY
Palomino Fino

BACKSTORY
This is just one of many excellent fino sherries I tasted this
year: several feature in *WoW 2020*. If you are a sherry-
lover, the choice has never been better!

162

Ten Year Old Malvasia, Barbeito, Madeira, NV
Portugal 19% **€39.99**

345

STOCKISTS: Wines on the Green, Dublin 2, celticwhiskeyshop.com.

Ten Year Old Malvasia, Barbeito, Madeira, NV

TASTING NOTE
Delectable smooth sweet peaches and honey with burnt orange and caramel.

DRINK WITH
On its own as a digestif after dinner, with foie gras, or with lighter desserts.

STYLE
Fortified Wines

GRAPE VARIETY
Malvasia

BACKSTORY
Madeira is a much-underrated wine; not only is it very keenly priced but having gone through the unique estufagem process, it keeps forever once opened. Perfect for that occasional nightcap!

163

Taylor's Finest Vintage Port 2017
Portugal 20% **€120**

STOCKISTS: Jus de Vine, Portmarnock, jusdevine.ie; Green Man Wines, Dublin 6, greenmanwines.ie; Mitchell & Son, Dublin 1, Sandycove, and Avoca, Kilmacanogue & Dunboyne, mitchellandson.com; Le Caveau, Kilkenny, lecaveau.ie.

Taylor's Finest Vintage Port 2017

TASTING NOTE

Wonderful aromas of violets and ripe damsons; the palate is closed, uncompromising and dense; with layers of ripe dark fruits; herbs and Christmas cake spice; poised, firm and tannic, this will improve for years to come. Glorious wine though.

DRINK WITH

Ideally vintage Port needs a minimum of five years, preferably ten before opening; then serve it with firm or blue cheese.

STYLE

Fortified Wines

GRAPE VARIETY

Touriga Nacional, Touriga Francesa, Tinto Cão, Tinta Roriz, Tinta Barroca

BACKSTORY

If you became a parent or god-parent in 2017, this would be the perfect gift to lay down for your daughter, son or godchild; it will certainly last longer than you - a good way to be remembered?

Leabharlanna Poiblí Chathair Baile Átha Cliath
Dublin City Public Libraries

INDEX OF WINES

Clos des Fous 'Pour ma Gueule" 2017, Itata Valley	218
Clos Saint Yves 2016 Savannières, Domaine des Baumard	114
Colle Morino 2017, Barba, Montepulciano d'Abruzzo	142
Corison Cabernet Sauvignon 2014, Napa Valley, California	330
Côtes du Rhône Saint-Esprit 2017, Delas	250
Cucú 2018, Barco del Corneta, Rueda	66
Custoza Boscroi 2018, Monte dei Roari	280
Cuvée Equinox 2017, Crozes-Hermitage, Domaine des Lises	224
D.O.C. Malbec 2016, Norton, Lujan de Cuyo, Mendoza	258
d'Arenberg Hermit Crab 2016, Mclaren Vale	98
Daniel Bouland Morgon Courcelette Vieilles Vignes 2016	232
Dedicace 2017, Lirac, Domaine Coudoulis	260
di Gino 2017, Rosso Piceno San Lorenzo	154
Domaine Bastide Neuve 2018, Rosé d'Oc	120
Domaine Desvignes Morgon 'La Voûte St-Vincent' 2017	178
Domaine Lardy Moulin-à-Vent Vieilles Vignes 2016	158
Drink Me Nat 'Cool' 2017, 1 litre bottle, Bairrada, Niepoort	168
Eggo Tinto de Tiza Malbec 2016, Viña Zorzal	230
El Maestro Sierra Fino	344
Etna Rosso Guardioloa 2016, Tenuta delle Terre Nere	306
Fleurie Tradition 2016, Domaine de la Madone	152
Folk Machine 'Parts & Labor' Red 2016, California	174
Framingham Pinot Noir 2016, Marlborough	180
Freisa d'Asti Secco 2015, Tenuta Olim Bauda	166
Friulano 2018, Volpe Pasini, Friuli Colli Orientale	62
Gabriela Pago Balbaina, Sanchez Ayala, Manzanilla	336
Gambellara Classico 2018, Cantina di Gambellara	64
Garzon Tannat Reserva 2017,	264
Giacomo Fenocchio Roero Arneis 2017	84
Gianni Brunelli Rosso di Montalcino 2017	274
Herdade de Grous Branco 2017, VR Alentejo	70
Imaginador 2017, Pedro Parra, Itata	234
Immich-Bateriberg Riesling Detonation 2017, Mosel	48
Ink 2018, Judith Beck, Burgenland	284
Iroulegy Tradition 2015, Domaine Arretxea	238
Jansz Tasmania Vintage Cuvée 2012	8
Jarrarte 2018 Rioja Joven, Abel Mendoza	252
Johanneshöhe Blaufränkisch 2017, Burgenland, Prieler	228
Julia Florista Branco, NV	56
Kershaw Clonal Selection Chardonnay 2017	116
Krug Grand Cuvee Brut N.V., Champagne	22
Kumeu River Estate Chardonnay 2018, Auckland	110
La Porte Saint Jean, Saumur 2015 , Sylvain Dittière	194
La Raspa Blanca Seco 2017, Bodegas Viñedos Verticales, Sierras de Malaga	40
La Roncière Pinot Noir 2017, Val de Loire, André Vatan	146

Langhe Nebbiolo 2016, Pian delle Mole, Giula Negri	268
Le Temps des C(e)rises 2014, Santenay, Domaine Olivier	184
Le Vin est une Fête 2017, Côtes du Marmandais, Elian da Ros	144
Leirana, Albariño, Forjas del Salnes 2018, Rías Baixas	82
Les Secrets de Sophie Touraine Sauvignon Blanc 2018	36
Les Vignes d'Oc Rouge Grenache / Merlot 2018, Languedoc	204
Lomba des Ares 2016, Ribeira Sacra, Fedellos do Couto	186
M&S Cava Brut NV	4
Marks & Spencer Manzanilla	334
Marzemino 2018 Roberta Fugatti, IGT Marzemino della Vallagarina	140
Masetto Nero 2016, Endrizzi, Vigneti delle Dolomiti	164
Merinas Old Vine Tempranillo 2018, Bodegas Fontana, Uclés	242
Mimetic 2018, Gallinas de Piel, Calatayud	262
Mitchell & Son Claret 2015, Bordeaux Superieur	134
Montes Outer Limits "Old Roots" Cinsault 2018, Itata	222
Muros Antigos Vinho Verde 2018	28
Muscadet de Sèvre & Maine sur lie, La Louvetrie 2018	38
Old Vine Reserve Chenin Blanc 2018, Ken Forrester Vineyards, Stellenbosch	100
Oloroso, Marqués de Poley , Montilla-Moriles, Toro Albala	340
Passo Sardo 2016, Cannonau di Sardegna	246
Pavillon de Léoville Poyferré 2015, St. Julien	310
Petit Chardonnay 2018, Ken Forrester Wines, Western Cape	60
Petit Sao 2015, Costers del Segre	248
Pheasant's Tears Saperavi 2018	288
Piedradolce Etna Bianco 2018	88
Pinot Noir Les Petits Apotres 2018, Domaine de Bon Augures	156
Pinot Noir, Domaine de la Renne, Val de Loire	132
Pretty Pony 2013, Kanaan Winery, Ningxia Helan Mountain	318
Quinta de Saes Tobias Encruzado, Dao 2018	102
Quinta de Saes Tobias Tinto, Dao 2016	148
Reminat Primitivo 2018, IGT Terre di Chieti	256
Réserve de Boulas Laudun Côtes du Rhône Villages 2018	96
Réserve du Boulas Côtes du Rhône Rosé 2018	122
Reto 2018, Manchuela, Bodegas Ponce	78
Rioja Reserva 2012, La Granja Nuestra Senora de Remelluri, Remelluri	270
Rivera del Notro 2017, Itata, Roberto Henriques	290
Roka Furmint 2018, Kog, Stajerska	42
Rosso Piceno 2017, Saladini Pilastri	136
Rosso Piceno DOC, Cantina dei Colli Ripani 2018	208
Rouge-Gorge 2017, Coteaux de Loir Domaine de Bellivière	192
Ruinart R de Ruinart Champagne NV	12
Sancerre Rouge La Croix du Roy 2014, Lucien Crochet	188
Sandhi Pinot Noir 2016, Sta. Rita Hills, California	300
Sandhi Sanford & Benedict Chardonnay 2016	320

Santa Rita 120 Cabernet Franc	200
Seleccion de Bodega Malbec 2016, Dona Paula, Alluvia Vineyard, Gualtallary	272
Sherazadze Donnafugatta 2018, Sicilia DOC, Nero d'Avola	220
Silice 2017, Ribera Sacra	176
Soalheiro Alvarinho 2018, Monçao & Melgaço, Vinho Verde	46
Solto Escola 2016, Vinho Verde, Portugal	26
St. Joseph 'Grand Duc du Montillet' 2017, Domaine du Monteillet	92
T'Air Syrah, Pays d'Oc 2017	206
Tahbilk Marsanne 2018, Nagambie Lakes, Central Victoria	30
Taylor's Finest Vintage Port 2017	348
Taylor's Late-Bottled Vintage Port 2014	342
Ten Year Old Malvasia, Barbeito, Madeira, NV	346
Terlaner Cuvée 2018, Trentino	80
Terrasse 2017, Keermont, Stellenbosch	108
Terroir Unico Chardonnay 2018, Vina Zorzal	72
Tesco Finest Côtes de Gascogne 2018	54
The Flower and the Bee, Ribeiro, Coto de Gomariz 2018	44
Tolloy Blauburgunder / Pino Nero 2017 Sud Tirol-Alto Adige	150
Tolpuddle Vineyard Pinot Noir 2015, Coal River, Tasmania	328
Trefiano 2015, Carmignano Riserva 2015, Cappezzana	324
Trenzado 2018, Bodegas Suerte del Marqués, Tenerife	50
Two Paddocks 'The Fusilier' Pinot Noir 2018, Central Otago	322
Unlitro 2018, Ampelia IGT Costa Toscana	294
Verdicchio dei Castelli di Jeso Classico Superiore Capovolto 2018, La Marca di San Michele	292
Vermentino di Sardegna 2018, Sella & Mosca	58
Viano 'Hillside" Red NV	216
Viña Tondonia 2005, Bodegas Lopez de Heredia, Rioja Reserva Blanco	308
Viré-Clessé 2017, Les Pierres Blanches, Domaine André Bonhomme	104
Vola Vole 2018, Trebbiano d'Abruzzo	286
Volcánico País 2018, A los Viñateros Bravos, Itata	160
Wildflower Pinot Noir 2018	130
Zephyr 2017, Les Deux Cols, Cotes du Rhone	106

INDEX OF STOCKISTS

STOCKISTS CONTINUED

	Style	Price	Wine No.
Herdade de Grous Branco 2017, VR Alentejo	White	€18	32
Terroir Unico Chardonnay 2018, Vina Zorzal	White	€18.50	33
Reto 2018, Manchuela, Bodegas Ponce	White	€21	36
St. Joseph 'Grand Duc du Montillet' 2017, Monteillet	White	€38	43
Adèle 2018, Eric Texier,	White	€23-26	40
Drink Me Nat 'Cool' 2017, 1 litre bottle, Bairrada, Niepoort	Red	€25	78
Sherazadze Donnafugatta 2018, Nero d'Avola	Red	€23	103
Montes Outer Limits "Old Roots" Cinsault 2018, Itata	Red	€23.99	104
Mimetic 2018, Gallinas de Piel, Calatayud	Red	€19.99	123
Garzon Tannat Reserva 2017,	Red	€20	124
Rioja Reserva 2012, Senora de Remelluri, Remelluri	Red	€32	127
Ink 2018, Judith Beck, Burgenland	Red	€17.95	133
Unlitro 2018, Ampelia IGT Costa Toscana	Red	€24.50	138
Chablis 1er cru Vauleront 2015, La Chablisienne	White	€40	141
Viña Tondonia 2005, Bodegas Lopez de Heredia, Rioja Reserva Blanco	White	€45	144
As Sortes 2017, Rafael Palacios, Valdeorras	White	€46	146
Tolpuddle Vineyard Pinot Noir 2015, Tasmania	Red	€62.99	154
Callejuela Manzanilla Fina NV	Fortified	€18	158

Blackrock Cellar, Co Dublin, blackrockcellar.com;

	Style	Price	Wine No.
Charles Heidsieck Brut Réserve Champagne	Sparkling	€70	8
Friulano 2018, Volpe Pasini, Friuli Colli Orientale	White	€15.50	28
Cucú 2018, Barco del Corneta, Rueda	White	€17.75	30
Amalaya Torrontés Riesling 2018, Calchaquí Valley	White	€17.99	31
Reto 2018, Manchuela, Bodegas Ponce	White	€21.00	36
Leirana, Albariño, Forjas del Salnes 2018, Rías Baixas	White	€25	38
Viré-Clessé 2017, Les Pierres Blanches, André Bonhomme	White	€22.95	48
Volcánico País 2018, A los Viñateros Bravos, Itata	Red	€23.85	74
Cielo Rosso 2018 IGP Terre Siciliane	Red	€12.95	94
Clos des Fous 'Pour ma Gueule" 2017, Itata Valley	Red	€19.99	102

STOCKISTS CONTINUED

	Style	Price	Wine No.
Montes Outer Limits "Old Roots" Cinsault 2018, Itata	Red	€23.99	104
Johanneshöhe Blaufränkisch 2017, Burgenland, Prieler	Red	€25	107
Eggo Tinto de Tiza Malbec 2016, Viña Zorzal	Red	€25	108
Mimetic 2018, Gallinas de Piel, Calatayud	Red	€19.99	123
Garzon Tannat Reserva 2017,	Red		€20
124 Rioja Reserva 2012, Senora de Remelluri, Remelluri	Red	€32	127
Bardolino "Reboi" 2018, Monte dei Roari	Red	€17	132
Rivera del Notro 2017, Itata, Roberto Henriques	White	€24	136
Unlitro 2018, Ampelia IGT Costa Toscana	Red	€24.50	138
Sandhi Pinot Noir 2016, Sta. Rita Hills, California	Red	€38	140
Etna Rosso Guardioloa 2016, Tenuta delle Terre Nere	Red	€45	143
Viña Tondonia 2005, Bodegas Lopez de Heredia, Rioja Reserva Blanco	White	€45	144
As Sortes 2017, Rafael Palacios, Valdeorras	White	€46	146
Sandhi Sanford & Benedict Chardonnay 2016	White	€50	150
Tolpuddle Vineyard Pinot Noir 2015, Tasmania	Red	€62.99	154
Callejuela Manzanilla Fina NV	Fortified	€18	158

Bradleys Off-licence, Cork, bradleysofflicence.ie

	Style	Price	Wine No.
Bollinger Special Cuvée Champagne NV	Sparkling	€55.65	4
Ruinart R de Ruinart Champagne NV	Sparkling	€58.40	5
Ch.du Coing de St. Fiacre 2017, Muscadet	White	€16.55	15
Leirana, Albariño, Forjas del Salnes 2018, Rías Baixas	White	€25	38
d'Arenberg Hermit Crab 2016, Mclaren Vale	White	€16.95	45
Cielo Rosso 2018 IGP Terre Siciliane	Red	€12.95	94
Passo Sardo 2016, Cannonau di Sardegna	Red	€14.00	115
Côtes du Rhône Saint-Esprit 2017, Delas	Red	€16.95	117
Mimetic 2018, Gallinas de Piel, Calatayud	Red	€19.99	123
Ink 2018, Judith Beck, Burgenland	Red	€17.95	133
Pheasant's Tears Saperavi 2018	Red	€23.95	135
Unlitro 2018, Ampelia IGT Costa Toscana	Red	€24.50	138

STOCKISTS CONTINUED	Style	Price	Wine No.
Butler & Byrne, Cong.			
Roka Furmint 2018, Kog, Stajerska	White	€19.50	19
Cabot and Co., Westport, Cabotandco.com			
Roka Furmint 2018, Kog, Stajerska	White	€19.50	19
Pinot Noir Les Petits Apotres 2018, Dom. de Bon Augures	Red	€22	72
Les Vignes d'Oc Rouge Grenache / Merlot 2018	Red	€12.99	95
Daniel Bouland Morgon Courcelette Vieilles Vignes 2016	Red	€26	109
Jarrarte 2018 Rioja Joven, Abel Mendoza	Red	€17	118
Cashel Wine Cellar, cashel.ie			
Sherazadze Donnafugatta 2018, Nero d'Avola	Red	€23	103
Chablis 1er cru Vauleront 2015, La Chablisienne	White	€40	141
Two Paddocks 'The Fusilier' Pinot Noir 2018,	Red	€50	151
Cass & Co. Dungarvan, Cassandco.ie			
Ink 2018, Judith Beck, Burgenland	Red	€17.95	133
Unlitro 2018, Ampelia IGT Costa Toscana	Red	€24.50	138
The Cinnamon Cottage, Cork, cinnamoncottage.ie			
Altos Las Hormigas Tinto 2017, Mendoza	Red	€17.99	100
Mimetic 2018, Gallinas de Piel, Calatayud	Red	€19.99	123
Bodega Colomé 'Auténtico' Salta Malbec 2017	Red	€41.99	142
Clontarf Wines, Dublin 3 clontarfwines.ie			
Bollinger Special Cuvée Champagne NV	Sparkling	€55.65	4
Charles Heidsieck Brut Réserve Champagne	Sparkling	€70	8
The Flower and the Bee, Ribeiro, Gomariz	White	€19.95	20
Terroir Unico Chardonnay 2018, Vina Zorzal	White	€18.50	33
Quinta de Saes Tobias Encruzado, Dao 2018	White	€18.95	47
Quinta de Saes Tobias Tinto, Dao 2016	Red	€18.95	68
Cielo Rosso 2018 IGP Terre Siciliane	Red	€12.95	94
Altos Las Hormigas Tinto 2017, Mendoza	Red	€17.99	100
Eggo Tinto de Tiza Malbec 2016, Viña Zorzal	Red	€25	108
Passo Sardo 2016, Cannonau di Sardegna	Red	€14	115
Garzon Tannat Reserva 2017,	Red	€20	124
Rioja Reserva 2012, Senora de Remelluri, Remelluri	Red	€32	127
Ink 2018, Judith Beck, Burgenland	Red	€17.95	133
Viña Tondonia 2005, Bodegas Lopez de Heredia, Rioja Reserva Blanco	White	€45	144

STOCKISTS CONTINUED	Style	Price	Wine No.
As Sortes 2017, Rafael Palacios, Valdeorras	White	€46	146
Taylor's Late-Bottled Vintage Port 2014	Fortified	€24	160

The Coach House, Dublin 14, thecoachhouseofflicence.ie

	Style	Price	Wine No.
La Raspa Blanca 2017, Bodegas Viñedos Verticales, Malaga	White	€19	18
Beaujolais '69' 2017, Christophe Coquard	Red	€16	63
Domaine Lardy Moulin-à-Vent Vieilles Vignes 2016	Red	€22	73
Rivera del Notro 2017, Itata, Roberto Henriques	White	€24	136

Coolers, Swords

	Style	Price	Wine No.
Côtes du Rhône Saint-Esprit 2017, Delas	Red	€16.95	117

The Corkscrew, Dublin 2, thecorkscrew.ie

	Style	Price	Wine No.
Bollinger Special Cuvée Champagne NV	Sparkling	€55.65	4
Ruinart R de Ruinart Champagne NV	Sparkling	€58.40	5
Ch.du Coing de St. Fiacre 2017, Muscadet	White	€16.55	15
Soalheiro Alvarinho 2018, Vinho Verde	White	€21	21
Cucú 2018, Barco del Corneta, Rueda	White	€17.75	30
Amalaya Torrontés Riesling 2018, Calchaquí Valley	White	€17.99	31
Herdade de Grous Branco 2017, VR Alentejo	White	€18	32
Reto 2018, Manchuela, Bodegas Ponce	White	€21.00	36
Leirana, Albariño, Forjas del Salnes 2018, Rías Baixas	White	€25	38
Terrasse 2017, Keermont, Stellenbosch	White	€30	50
Kumeu River Estate Chardonnay 2018, Auckland	White	€33.00	51
Kershaw Clonal Selection Chardonnay 2017	White	€54	54
Volcánico País 2018, A los Viñateros Bravos, Itata	Red	€23.85	74
Drink Me Nat 'Cool' 2017, 1 litre bottle, Bairrada, Niepoort	Red	€25	78
Framingham Pinot Noir 2016, Marlborough	Red	€27.99	84
Altos Las Hormigas Tinto 2017, Mendoza	Red	€17.99	100
Sherazadze Donnafugatta 2018, Nero d'Avola	Red	€23	103
Johanneshöhe Blaufränkisch 2017, Burgenland, Prieler	Red	€25	107
Côtes du Rhône Saint-Esprit 2017, Delas	Red	€16.95	117
Rioja Reserva 2012, Senora de Remelluri, Remelluri	Red	€32	127
Pheasant's Tears Saperavi 2018	Red	€23.95	135
Bodega Colomé 'Auténtico' Salta Malbec 2017	Red	€41.99	142
Viña Tondonia 2005, Bodegas Lopez de Heredia, Rioja Reserva Blanco	White	€45	144

STOCKISTS CONTINUED	Style	Price	Wine No.
As Sortes 2017, Rafael Palacios, Valdeorras	White	€46	146
Pretty Pony 2013, Kanaan Winery, Ningxia	Red	€49.99	149
Tolpuddle Vineyard Pinot Noir 2015, Tasmania	Red	€62.99	154
Callejuela Manzanilla Fina NV	Fortified	€18	158
El Maestro Sierra Fino	Fortified	€25.99	161

The Counter, Letterkenny.

Soalheiro Alvarinho 2018, Vinho Verde	White	€21	21
T'Air Syrah, Pays d'Oc 2017	Red	€14.50	96

Crafted, Bennettsbridge Kilkenny

The Flower and the Bee, Ribeiro, Gomariz	White	€19.95	20
Quinta de Saes Tobias Encruzado, Dao 2018	White	€18.95	47
Quinta de Saes Tobias Tinto, Dao 2016	Red	€18.95	68
Rosso Piceno DOC, Cantina dei Colli Ripani 2018	Red	€14.95	97

Daly's, Boyle, Co. Roscommon

Domaine Lardy Moulin-à-Vent Vieilles Vignes 2016	Red	€22	73

D-Six Wines, Dublin 6; peggykellys.ie.

Solto Escola 2016, Vinho Verde, Portugal	White	€13.95	11
Domaine Lardy Moulin-à-Vent Vieilles Vignes 2016	Red	€22	73
Ch. Bellevue-La-Forêt 2016, Fronton	Red	€16	99
Garzon Tannat Reserva 2017,	Red	€20	124

Deveney's, Dublin 14

Champagne Delamotte Blanc de Blancs NV	Sparkling	€60	6
The Flower and the Bee, Ribeiro, Gomariz	White	€19.95	20
Giacomo Fenocchio Roero Arneis 2017	White	€26	39
d'Arenberg Hermit Crab 2016, Mclaren Vale	White	€16.95	45
Quinta de Saes Tobias Encruzado, Dao 2018	White	€18.95	47
Zephyr 2017, Les Deux Cols, Cotes du Rhone	White	€22.95	49
Quinta de Saes Tobias Tinto, Dao 2016	Red	€18.95	68
Viano 'Hillside" Red NV	Red	€18	101
Chemin des Fonts 2018, Les Deux Cols, C. du Rhône	Red	€28.50	111
Garzon Tannat Reserva 2017,	Red	€20	124
Seleccion de Bodega Malbec 2016, Dona Paula	Red	€35	128
Benje Tinto, Envínate, 2017	Red	€28	139
Sandhi Pinot Noir 2016, Sta. Rita Hills, California	Red	€38	140
Chablis 1er cru Vauleront 2015,La Chablisienne	White	€40	141

Dollard & Co., Dublin 2, Dollardandco.ie

Champagne Lous Roederer Brut Premier NV	Sparkling	€62	7

STOCKISTS CONTINUED	Style	Price	Wine No.
Donnybrook Fair, donnybrookfair.ie			
Bollinger Special Cuvée Champagne	Sparkling	€55.65	4
Charles Heidsieck Brut Réserve Champagne	Sparkling	€70	8
d'Arenberg Hermit Crab 2016, Mclaren Vale	White	€16.95	45
T'Air Syrah, Pays d'Oc 2017	Red	€14.50	96
Ch. Bellevue-La-Forêt 2016, Fronton	Red	€16	99
Altos Las Hormigas Tinto 2017, Mendoza	Red	€17.99	100
Côtes du Rhône Saint-Esprit 2017, Delas	Red	€16.95	117
Bodega Colomé 'Auténtico' Salta Malbec 2017	Red	€41.99	142
Drinkstore, Dublin 7, drinkstore.ie			
Gambellara Classico 2018, Cantina di Gambellara	White	€15.95	29
Rosso Piceno 2017, Saladini Pilastri	Red	€15.95	62
Sherazadze Donnafugatta 2018, Nero d'Avola	Red	€23	103
Garzon Tannat Reserva 2017,	Red	€20	124
Ink 2018, Judith Beck, Burgenland	Red	€17.95	133
Dunnes Stores, Dunnesstores.com			
Domaine Bastide Neuve 2018, Rosé d'Oc	Rosé	€10.50	55
Château Roc de Villepreux 2016, Bordeaux Supérieur	Red	€10.50	58
Ch. Bellevue-La-Forêt 2016, Fronton	Red	€16	99
Dwans's Off Licence, Dublin 16			
Montes Outer Limits "Old Roots" Cinsault 2018, Itata	Red	€23.99	104
Egan's, Drogheda			
d'Arenberg Hermit Crab 2016, Mclaren Vale	White	€16.95	45
Eldon's, Clonmel			
Ch. Bellevue-La-Forêt 2016, Fronton	Red	€16	99
Eleven Deli, Greystones, Elevendeli.ie			
di Gino 2017, Rosso Piceno San Lorenzo	Red	€21.50	71
Ely 64, Glasthule, Ely64.com			
Bollinger Special Cuvée Champagne NV	Sparkling	€55.65	4
Ruinart R de Ruinart Champagne NV	Sparkling	€58.40	5
Charles Heidsieck Brut Réserve Champagne	Sparkling	€70	8
The Flower and the Bee, Ribeiro, Gomariz	White	€19.95	20
Soalheiro Alvarinho 2018, Vinho Verde	White	€21	21
Immich-Bateriberg Riesling Detonation 2017,	White	€26	22

STOCKISTS CONTINUED

	Style	Price	Wine No.
Trenzado 2018, Suerte del Marqués, Tenerife	White	€26	23
Gambellara Classico 2018, Cantina di Gambellara	White	€15.95	29
Cucú 2018, Barco del Corneta, Rueda	White	€17.75	30
Reto 2018, Manchuela, Bodegas Ponce	White	€21	36
Terlaner Cuvée 2018, Trentino	White	€24.75	37
Leirana, Albariño, Forjas del Salnes 2018, Rías Baixas	White	€25	38
Adèle 2018, Eric Texier,	White	€23-26	40
Zephyr 2017, Les Deux Cols, Cotes du Rhone	White	€22.95	49
Clos Saint Yves 2016 Savannières, Domaine des Baumard	White	€36.75	53
Kershaw Clonal Selection Chardonnay 2017	White	€54	54
Marzemino 2018 Roberta Fugatti, IGT	Red	€16	64
Colle Morino 2017, Barba, Montepulciano d'Abruzzo	Red	€16.50	65
Drink Me Nat 'Cool' 2017, 1 litre bottle, Bairrada, Niepoort	Red	€25	78
Camino Real 2017 Ribera Sacra, Guímaro	Red	€26	79
Domaine Desvignes Morgon 'La Voûte St-Vincent' 2017	Red	€27	83
Lomba des Ares 2016, Ribeira Sacra, Fedellos do Couto	Red	€31.00	87
Sancerre Rouge La Croix du Roy 2014, Lucien Crochet	Red	€34	88
Bourgogne Pinot Noir 2015, Sylvain Pataille	Red	€35	89
Rouge-Gorge 2017, Coteaux de Loir Domaine de Bellivière	Red	€39	90
Cielo Rosso 2018 IGP Terre Siciliane	Red	€12.95	94
T'Air Syrah, Pays d'Oc 2017	Red	€14.50	96
Rosso Piceno DOC, Cantina dei Colli Ripani 2018	Red	€14.95	97
Altos Las Hormigas Tinto 2017, Mendoza	Red	€17.99	100
Sherazadze Donnafugatta 2018, Nero d'Avola	Red	€23	103
Montes Outer Limits "Old Roots" Cinsault 2018, Itata	Red	€23.99	104
Daniel Bouland Morgon Courcelette Vieilles Vignes 2016	Red	€26	109
Chemin des Fonts 2018, Les Deux Cols, C. du Rhône	Red	€28.50	111
Passo Sardo 2016, Cannonau di Sardegna	Red	€14.00	115
Rioja Reserva 2012, Senora de Remelluri, Remelluri	Red	€32	127
Custoza Boscroi 2018, Monte dei Roari	White	€17	131
Bardolino "Reboi" 2018, Monte dei Roari	Red	€17	132
Ink 2018, Judith Beck, Burgenland	Red	€17.95	133

STOCKISTS CONTINUED	Style	Price	Wine No.
Verdicchio dei Castelli di Jesi 2018, San Michele	White	€24	137
Unlitro 2018, Ampelia IGT Costa Toscana	Red	€24.50	138
Viña Tondonia 2005, Bodegas Lopez de Heredia, Rioja Reserva Blanco	White	€45	144
As Sortes 2017, Rafael Palacios, Valdeorras	White	€46	146
Brunello di Montalcino 2014, Col d'Orcia	Red	€48	147
Sandhi Sanford & Benedict Chardonnay 2016	White	€50	150
Trefiano 2015, Carmignano Riserva 2015, Cappezzana	Red	€54.99	152
Tolpuddle Vineyard Pinot Noir 2015, Tasmania	Red	€62.99	154
Callejuela Manzanilla Fina NV	Fortified	€18	158

Ely Wine Store - Maynooth

	Style	Price	Wine No.
Charles Heidsieck Brut Réserve Champagne	Sparkling	€70	8
Gambellara Classico 2018, Cantina di Gambellara	White	€15.95	29
69 Arrobas 2017, Rías Baixas, Albamar	White	€34	42
Zephyr 2017, Les Deux Cols, Cotes du Rhone	White	€22.95	49
Clos Saint Yves 2016 Savannières, Domaine des Baumard	White	€36.75	53
Altos Las Hormigas Tinto 2017, Mendoza	Red	€17.99	100
Montes Outer Limits "Old Roots" Cinsault 2018, Itata	Red	€23.99	104
Imaginador 2017, Pedro Parra, Itata	Red	€26.99	110
Mimetic 2018, Gallinas de Piel, Calatayud	Red	€19.99	123
Garzon Tannat Reserva 2017,	Red	€20	124
Anthill Farms 2016 Syrah, Campbell Ranch, Sonoma Coast	Red	€40	130
2016 Chablis 1er Cru Mont de Milieu, Domaine Christophe	White	€49	148
Trefiano 2015, Carmignano Riserva 2015, Cappezzana	Red	€54.99	152
Tolpuddle Vineyard Pinot Noir 2015, Tasmania	Red	€62.99	154

Ennis Gourmet Store, Ennis, ennisgourmet.com

	Style	Price	Wine No.
Côtes du Rhône Saint-Esprit 2017, Delas	Red	€16.95	117

Fagan's, D9, Fagans.ie

	Style	Price	Wine No.
Ch. Bellevue-La-Forêt 2016, Fronton	Red	€16	99

Fallon & Byrne, Dublin 2, fallonandbyrne.com

	Style	Price	Wine No.
Charles Heidsieck Brut Réserve Champagne	Sparkling	€70	8
Ch.du Coing de St. Fiacre 2017, Muscadet	White	€16.55	15
Cucú 2018, Barco del Corneta, Rueda	White	€17.75	30
Volcánico País 2018, A los Viñateros Bravos, Itata	Red	€23.85	74

STOCKISTS CONTINUED	Style	Price	Wine No.
Bourgueil 2017 La Coudraye, Y. Amirault	Red	€24	75
Cielo Rosso 2018 IGP Terre Siciliane	Red	€12.95	94
Sherazadze Donnafugatta 2018, Nero d'Avola	Red	€23	103
Ink 2018, Judith Beck, Burgenland	Red	€17.95	133
Brunello di Montalcino 2014, Col d'Orcia	Red	€48	147

Fine Wines, Limerick

Passo Sardo 2016, Cannonau di Sardegna	Red	€14	115
Taylor's Late-Bottled Vintage Port 2014	Fortified	€24	160

First Draft Coffee & Wine, Dublin 8, Firstdraftcoffeeandwine.com

Clima 2016, Vale da Capucha IG Lisboa	White	€20	35
Beaujolais '69' 2017, Christophe Coquard	Red	€16	63
Folk Machine 'Parts & Labor' Red 2016, California	Red	€26	81
Langhe Nebbiolo 2016, Pian delle Mole, Giula Negri	Red	€27	126

Fresh Outlets, freshthegoodfoodmarket.ie

Herdade de Grous Branco 2017, VR Alentejo	White	€18	32
Adèle 2018, Eric Texier,	White	€23-26	40
Ch. Bellevue-La-Forêt 2016, Fronton	Red	€16	99

Gibney's, Malahide, gibneys.com

Krug Grand Cuvee Brut N.V., Champagne	Sparkling	€215	10
Cucú 2018, Barco del Corneta, Rueda	White	€17.75	30
Sherazadze Donnafugatta 2018, Nero d'Avola	Red	€23	103
Garzon Tannat Reserva 2017,	Red	€20	124
Two Paddocks 'The Fusilier' Pinot Noir 2018,	Red	€50	151
Taylor's Late-Bottled Vintage Port 2014	Fortified	€24	160

The Grape & Grain, Co. Dublin, Leopardstowninn.ie

Côtes du Rhône Saint-Esprit 2017, Delas	Red	€16.95	117

Grapevine, Dalkey, onthegrapevine.ie

Ruinart R de Ruinart Champagne NV	Sparkling	€58.40	5
Champagne Delamotte Blanc de Blancs NV	Sparkling	€60	6
Champagne Lous Roederer Brut Premier NV	Sparkling	€62	7
Krug Grand Cuvee Brut N.V., Champagne	Sparkling	€215	10
Roka Furmint 2018, Kog, Stajerska	White	€19.50	19
d'Arenberg Hermit Crab 2016, Mclaren Vale	White	€16.95	45
Beaujolais '69' 2017, Christophe Coquard	Red	€16	63
Pinot Noir Les Petits Apotres 2018, Dom. de Bon Augures	Red	€22	72

STOCKISTS CONTINUED	Style	Price	Wine No.
Domaine Lardy Moulin-à-Vent Vieilles Vignes 2016	Red	€22	73
Les Vignes d'Oc Rouge Grenache / Merlot 2018	Red	€12.99	95
Viano 'Hillside" Red NV	Red	€18	101
Clos des Fous 'Pour ma Gueule" 2017, Itata Valley	Red	€19.99	102
Daniel Bouland Morgon Courcelette Vieilles Vignes 2016	Red	€26	109
Côtes du Rhône Saint-Esprit 2017, Delas	Red	€16.95	117
Jarrarte 2018 Rioja Joven, Abel Mendoza	Red	€17.00	118
Sandhi Pinot Noir 2016, Sta. Rita Hills, California	Red	€38	140

Green Man Wines, Terenure, greenmanwines.ie

	Style	Price	Wine No.
Charles Heidsieck Brut Réserve Champagne	Sparkling	€70	8
Ancre Hill Blanc de Noir N.V., Monmouth	Sparkling	€70	9
Ch.du Coing de St. Fiacre 2017, Muscadet	White	€16.55	15
The Flower and the Bee, Ribeiro, Gomariz	White	€19.95	20
Immich-Bateriberg Riesling Detonation 2017,	White	€26	22
Trenzado 2018, Suerte del Marqués, Tenerife	White	€26	23
Cucú 2018, Barco del Corneta, Rueda	White	€17.75	30
Reto 2018, Manchuela, Bodegas Ponce	White	€21	36
Leirana, Albariño, Forjas del Salnes 2018, Rías Baixas	White	€25	39
Giacomo Fenocchio Roero Arneis 2017	White	€26	39
Piedradolce Etna Bianco 2018	White	€27	41
69 Arrobas 2017, Rías Baixas, Albamar	White	€34	42
Adèle 2018, Eric Texier,	White	€23-26	40
Quinta de Saes Tobias Encruzado, Dao 2018	White	€18.95	47
Marzemino 2018 Roberta Fugatti, IGT	Red	€16.00	64
Quinta de Saes Tobias Tinto, Dao 2016	Red	€18.95	68
di Gino 2017, Rosso Piceno San Lorenzo	Red	€21.50	71
Volcánico País 2018, A los Viñateros Bravos, Itata	Red	€23.85	74
Bourgueil 2017 La Coudraye, Y. Amirault	Red	€24	75
Drink Me Nat 'Cool' 2017, 1 litre bottle, Bairrada, Niepoort	Red	€25	78
Camino Real 2017 Ribera Sacra, Guímaro	Red	€26	79
Domaine Desvignes Morgon 'La Voûte St-Vincent' 2017	Red	€27	83
Framingham Pinot Noir 2016, Marlborough	Red	€27.99	84
Lomba des Ares 2016, Ribeira Sacra, Fedellos do Couto	Red	€31	85
Sancerre Rouge La Croix du Roy 2014, Lucien Crochet	Red	€34	88

STOCKISTS CONTINUED	Style	Price	Wine No.
Rouge-Gorge 2017, Coteaux de Loir Domaine de Bellivière	Red	€39	90
Cielo Rosso 2018 IGP Terre Siciliane	Red	€12.95	94
Altos Las Hormigas Tinto 2017, Mendoza	Red	€17.99	100
Clos des Fous 'Pour ma Gueule" 2017, Itata Valley	Red	€19.99	102
Cuvée Equinox 2017, Crozes-Hermitage, Dom. des Lises	Red	€24	105
Eggo Tinto de Tiza Malbec 2016, Viña Zorzal	Red	€25	108
Passo Sardo 2016, Cannonau di Sardegna	Red	€14	115
Rioja Reserva 2012, Senora de Remelluri, Remelluri	Red	€32	127
Gianni Brunelli Rosso di Montalcino 2017	Red	€38	129
Ink 2018, Judith Beck, Burgenland	Red	€17.95	133
Pheasant's Tears Saperavi 2018	Red	€23.95	135
Rivera del Notro 2017, Itata, Roberto Henriques	White	€24	136
Unlitro 2018, Ampelia IGT Costa Toscana	Red	€24.50	138
Benje Tinto, Envínate, 2017	Red	€28	139
Viña Tondonia 2005, Bodegas Lopez de Heredia, Rioja Reserva Blanco	White	€45	144
As Sortes 2017, Rafael Palacios, Valdeorras	White	€46	146
Brunello di Montalcino 2014, Col d'Orcia	Red	€48.00	147
Corison Cabernet Sauvignon 2014, Napa Valley, California	Red	€132	155
Callejuela Manzanilla Fina NV	Fortified	€18	158
Taylor's Late-Bottled Vintage Port 2014	Fortified	€24	160
El Maestro Sierra Fino	Fortified	€25.99	161
Taylor's Finest Vintage Port 2017	Fortified	€120	163

Higgins OffLicence, Dublin 14, www.higginsofflicence.ie

	Style	Price	Wine No.
Drink Me Nat 'Cool' 2017, 1 litre bottle, Bairrada, Niepoort	Red	€25	78
Ch. Bellevue-La-Forêt 2016, Fronton	Red	€16	99
Côtes du Rhône Saint-Esprit 2017, Delas	Red	€16.95	117
Garzon Tannat Reserva 2017,	Red	€20	124

Il Fornaio Enoteca, Liffey Street, Dublin 1

	Style	Price	Wine No.
Terlaner Cuvée 2018, Trentino	White	€24.75	37
Masetto Nero 2016, Endrizzi, Vigneti delle Dolomiti	Red	€24.95	76

JNwine.com

	Style	Price	Wine No.
Soalheiro Alvarinho 2018, Vinho Verde	White	€21	21
T'Air d'OCN Syrah, Pays d'Oc 2017	Red	€14.50	96

STOCKISTS CONTINUED	Style	Price	Wine No.
Joyce's Supermarket, Joycesupermarket.ie			
Champagne Lous Roederer Brut Premier NV	Sparkling	€62	7
Passo Sardo 2016, Cannonau di Sardegna	Red	€14	115
Taylor's Late-Bottled Vintage Port 2014	Fortified	€24	160
Jus de Vine, Portmarnock, jusdevine.ie			
Ruinart R de Ruinart Champagne NV	Sparkling	€58.40	5
Charles Heidsieck Brut Réserve Champagne	Sparkling	€70	8
Krug Grand Cuvee Brut N.V., Champagne	Sparkling	€215	10
Cucú 2018, Barco del Corneta, Rueda	White	€17.75	30
Amalaya Torrontés Riesling 2018, Calchaquí Valley	White	€17.99	31
Reto 2018, Manchuela, Bodegas Ponce	White	€21.00	36
Sherazadze Donnafugatta 2018, Nero d'Avola	Red	€23	103
Passo Sardo 2016, Cannonau di Sardegna	Red	€14	115
Mimetic 2018, Gallinas de Piel, Calatayud	Red	€19.99	123
Rioja Reserva 2012, Senora de Remelluri, Remelluri	Red	€32	127
Seleccion de Bodega Malbec 2016, Dona Paula	Red	€35	128
Chablis 1er cru Vauleront 2015,La Chablisienne	White	€40	141
Viña Tondonia 2005, Bodegas Lopez de Heredia, Rioja Reserva Blanco	White	€45	144
Tolpuddle Vineyard Pinot Noir 2015, Tasmania	Red	€62.99	154
Callejuela Manzanilla Fina NV	Fortified	€18	158
Taylor's Late-Bottled Vintage Port 2014	Fortified	€24	160
Taylor's Finest Vintage Port 2017	Fortified	€120	163
Kellys, Dublin 3, kellysofflicence.ie			
The Flower and the Bee, Ribeiro, Gomariz	White	€19.95	20
Amalaya Torrontés Riesling 2018, Calchaquí Valley	White	€17.99	31
d'Arenberg Hermit Crab 2016, Mclaren Vale	White	€16.95	45
Quinta de Saes Tobias Encruzado, Dao 2018	White	€18.95	47
Quinta de Saes Tobias Tinto, Dao 2016	Red	€18.95	68
Rosso Piceno DOC, Cantina dei Colli Ripani 2018	Red	€14.95	97
Passo Sardo 2016, Cannonau di Sardegna	Red	€14.00	115
Côtes du Rhône Saint-Esprit 2017, Delas	Red	€16.95	117
Garzon Tannat Reserva 2017,	Red	€20	124
Taylor's Late-Bottled Vintage Port 2014	Fortified	€24	160

STOCKISTS CONTINUED

	Style	Price	Wine No.
La Touche Wines, Greystones, latouchewines4u.ie			
Charles Heidsieck Brut Réserve Champagne	Sparkling	€70	8
The Flower and the Bee, Ribeiro, Gomariz	White	€19.95	20
Herdade de Grous Branco 2017, VR Alentejo	White	€18	32
Terroir Unico Chardonnay 2018, Vina Zorzal	White	€18.50	33
d'Arenberg Hermit Crab 2016, Mclaren Vale	White	€16.95	45
Domaine Desvignes Morgon 'La Voûte St-Vincent' 2017	Red	€27	83
Ch. Bellevue-La-Forêt 2016, Fronton	Red	€16	99
Eggo Tinto de Tiza Malbec 2016, Viña Zorzal	Red	€25	108
Viña Tondonia 2005, Bodegas Lopez de Heredia, Rioja Reserva Blanco	White	€45	144
As Sortes 2017, Rafael Palacios, Valdeorras	White	€46	146
Le Caveau, Kilkenny, Lecaveau.ie			
Ch. du Coing de St. Fiacre 2017, Muscadet	White	€16.55	15
Viré-Clessé 2017, Les Pierres Blanches, André Bonhomme	White	€22.95	48
Volcánico País 2018, A los Viñateros Bravos, Itata	Red	€23.85	74
Ink 2018, Judith Beck, Burgenland	Red	€17.95	133
Pheasant's Tears Saperavi 2018	Red	€23.95	135
Unlitro 2018, Ampelia IGT Costa Toscana	Red	€24.50	138
Gabriela Pago Balbaina, Manzanilla	Fortified	€12.30*	157
Taylor's Late-Bottled Vintage Port 2014	Fortified	€24	160
Taylor's Finest Vintage Port 2017	Fortified	€120	163
Lilliput Stores, Dublin 7, lilliputstores.com			
La Raspa Blanca 2017, Bodegas Viñedos Verticales, Malaga	White	€19	18
Immich-Bateriberg Riesling Detonation 2017,	White	€26	22
Cucú 2018, Barco del Corneta, Rueda	White	€17.75	30
Listons, Camden St., listonsfoodstore.ie			
Ch.du Coing de St. Fiacre 2017, Muscadet	White	€16.55	15
Viré-Clessé 2017, Les Pierres Blanches, André Bonhomme	White	€22.95	48
Rosso Piceno 2017, Saladini Pilastri	Red	€15.95	62
Loose Canon, Dublin 2, loosecanon.ie			
Immich-Bateriberg Riesling Detonation 2017,	White	€26	22
Trenzado 2018, Suerte del Marqués, Tenerife	White	€26	23
Clima 2016, Vale da Capucha IG Lisboa	White	€20	35

*per 1/2 bottle

STOCKISTS CONTINUED	Style	Price	Wine No.
Drink Me Nat 'Cool' 2017, 1 litre bottle, Bairrada, Niepoort	Red	€25	78
Lomba des Ares 2016, Ribeira Sacra, Fedellos do Couto	Red	€31	85
Ink 2018, Judith Beck, Burgenland	Red	€17.95	133
Rivera del Notro 2017, Itata, Roberto Henriques	White	€24	136
Unlitro 2018, Ampelia IGT Costa Toscana	Red	€24.50	138

MacGuinness Wines, Dundalk, dundalkwines.com
	Style	Price	Wine No.
Ch.du Coing de St. Fiacre 2017, Muscadet	White	€16.55	15
Herdade de Grous Branco 2017, VR Alentejo	White	€18	32
Viré-Clessé 2017, Les Pierres Blanches, André Bonhomme	White	€22.95	48
Passo Sardo 2016, Cannonau di Sardegna	Red	€14.00	115
Garzon Tannat Reserva 2017,	Red	€20	124
Taylor's Late-Bottled Vintage Port 2014	Fortified	€24	160

Market 57, Westport.
	Style	Price	Wine No.
Daniel Bouland Morgon Courcelette Vieilles Vignes 2016	Red	€26	109
Jarrarte 2018 Rioja Joven, Abel Mendoza	Red	€17	118

Marks & Spencer, Marksandspencer.com
	Style	Price	Wine No.
M&S Cava Brut NV	Sparkling	€10.50	1
Réserve de Boulas Laudun Côtes du Rhône Villages 2018	White	€13.30	44
Réserve du Boulas C. du Rhône Rosé 2018	Rosé	€13.30	56
Merinas Old Vine Tempranillo 2 018, Fontana, Uclés	Red	€10.50	113
Marks & Spencer Manzanilla	Fortified	€12	156

Martin's Off-Licence, Dublin 3, martinsofflicence.ie
	Style	Price	Wine No.
Charles Heidsieck Brut Réserve Champagne	Sparkling	€70	8
Gambellara Classico 2018, Cantina di Gambellara	White	€15.95	29
Cucú 2018, Barco del Corneta, Rueda	White	€17.75	30
Amalaya Torrontés Riesling 2018, Calchaquí Valley	White	€17.99	31
Reto 2018, Manchuela, Bodegas Ponce	White	€21	36
d'Arenberg Hermit Crab 2016, Mclaren Vale	White	€16.95	45
Zephyr 2017, Les Deux Cols, Cotes du Rhone	White	€22.95	49
Domaine Lardy Moulin-à-Vent Vieilles Vignes 2016	Red	€22	73
Ch. Bellevue-La-Forêt 2016, Fronton	Red	€16	99

STOCKISTS CONTINUED

	Style	Price	Wine No.
Clos des Fous 'Pour ma Gueule" 2017, Itata Valley	Red	€19.99	102
Sherazadze Donnafugatta 2018, Nero d'Avola	Red	€23	103
Mimetic 2018, Gallinas de Piel, Calatayud	Red	€19.99	123
Rioja Reserva 2012, Senora de Remelluri, Remelluri	Red	€32	127
Ink 2018, Judith Beck, Burgenland	Red	€17.95	133
Viña Tondonia 2005, Bodegas Lopez de Heredia, Rioja Reserva Blanco	White	€45	144
Callejuela Manzanilla Fina NV	Fortified	€18	158

Matson's, Grange and Bandon, matsonswinesandbeer.com

	Style	Price	Wine No.
Herdade de Grous Branco 2017, VR Alentejo	White	€18	32

McCabes Wines, Dublin 18, mccabeswines.ie.

	Style	Price	Wine No.
Muros Antigos Vinho Verde 2018	White	€14	12

McCambridges, Galway, Mccambridges.com

	Style	Price	Wine No.
Ruinart R de Ruinart Champagne NV	Sparkling	€58.40	5
Terroir Unico Chardonnay 2018, Vina Zorzal	White	€18.50	33

McHughs, Dublin 5, mchughs.ie

	Style	Price	Wine No.
Passo Sardo 2016, Cannonau di Sardegna	Red	€14	115
Chablis 1er cru Vauleront 2015,La Chablisienne	White	€40	141
Taylor's Late-Bottled Vintage Port 2014	Fortified	€24	160

Michael's of Mount Merrion, Michaels.ie

	Style	Price	Wine No.
Amalaya Torrontés Riesling 2018, Calchaquí Valley	White	€17.99	31
Montes Outer Limits "Old Roots" Cinsault 2018, Itata	Red	€23.99	104

Mitchell & Son, Dublin 1, Sandycove, and Avoca, Kilmacanogue & Dunboyne mitchellandson.com

	Style	Price	Wine No.
Bollinger Special Cuvée Champagne NV	Sparkling	€55.65	4
Ruinart R de Ruinart Champagne NV	Sparkling	€58.40	5
Champagne Delamotte Blanc de Blancs NV	Sparkling	€60	6
Charles Heidsieck Brut Réserve Champagne	Sparkling	€70	8
Krug Grand Cuvee Brut N.V., Champagne	Sparkling	€215	10
Viré-Clessé 2017, Les Pierres Blanches, André Bonhomme	White	€22.95	48
Kershaw Clonal Selection Chardonnay 2017	White	€54	54
Mitchell & Son Claret 2015, Bordeaux Superieur	Red	€15	61

STOCKISTS CONTINUED	Style	Price	Wine No.
Tolloy Blauburgunder / Pino Nero 2017 Sud Tirol-Alto Adige	Red	€18.95	69
Fleurie Tradition 2016, Domaine de la Madone	Red	€20.95	70
Freisa d'Asti Secco 2015, Tenuta Olim Bauda	Red	€24.95	77
Drink Me Nat 'Cool' 2017, 1 litre bottle, Bairrada, Niepoort	Red	€25	78
Sancerre Rouge La Croix du Roy 2014, Lucien Crochet	Red	€34	88
Cuvée Equinox 2017, Crozes-Hermitage, Dom. des Lises	Red	€24	105
Anthill Farms 2016 Syrah, Campbell Ranch, Sonoma Coast	Red	€40	130
Brunello di Montalcino 2014, Col d'Orcia	Red	€48	147
Pretty Pony 2013, Kanaan Winery, Ningxia	Red	€49.99	149
Barolo Castiglione 2015, Vietti, Piemonte	Red	€55	153
Tolpuddle Vineyard Pinot Noir 2015, Tasmania	Red	€62.99	154
Taylor's Late-Bottled Vintage Port 2014	Fortified	€24	160
Taylor's Finest Vintage Port 2017	Fortified	€120	163

Molloy's Liquor Stores, molloys.ie

Ch. Bellevue-La-Forêt 2016, Fronton	Red	€16	99
Côtes du Rhône Saint-Esprit 2017, Delas	Red	€16.95	117

Morton's, Dublin 6, mortons.ie

Herdade de Grous Branco 2017, VR Alentejo	White	€18	32
d'Arenberg Hermit Crab 2016, Mclaren Vale	White	€16.95	45
Kumeu River Estate Chardonnay 2018, Auckland	White	€33	51
di Gino 2017, Rosso Piceno San Lorenzo	Red	€21.50	71
Ch. Bellevue-La-Forêt 2016, Fronton	Red	€16.00	99

Mortons of Galway, Mortonsofgalway.ie

Rosso Piceno 2017, Saladini Pilastri	Red	€15.95	62
Domaine Lardy Moulin-à-Vent Vieilles Vignes 2016	Red	€22	73
Côtes du Rhône Saint-Esprit 2017, Delas	Red	€16.95	117

Myles Doyle, Gorey

Mitchell & Son Claret 2015, Bordeaux Superieur	Red	€15	61
Fleurie Tradition 2016, Domaine de la Madone	Red	€20.95	70

Nolan's, Dublin 3, nolans.ie

Muros Antigos Vinho Verde 2018	White	€14.00	12
Côtes du Rhône Saint-Esprit 2017, Delas	Red	€16.95	117

	Style	Price	Wine No.
STOCKISTS CONTINUED			

No.1 Pery Square, Limerick, Oneperysquare.com

	Style	Price	Wine No.
Pinot Noir Les Petits Apotres 2018, Dom. de Bon Augures	Red	€22	72
Les Vignes d'Oc Rouge Grenache / Merlot 2018	Red	€12.99	95
Daniel Bouland Morgon Courcelette Vieilles Vignes 2016	Red	€26	109

O'Briens, obrienswine.ie

	Style	Price	Wine No.
Jansz Tasmania Vintage Cuvée 2012	Sparkling	€35	3
Bollinger Special Cuvée Champagne NV	Sparkling	€55.65	4
Ruinart R de Ruinart Champagne NV	Sparkling	€58.40	5
Champagne Lous Roederer Brut Premier NV	Sparkling	€62	7
Charles Heidsieck Brut Réserve Champagne	Sparkling	€70	8
Krug Grand Cuvee Brut N.V., Champagne	Sparkling	€215	10
Arinto 2018, Vinho Verde, Quinta Picouto de Cima	White	€14.95	14
Les Secrets de Sophie Touraine Sauvignon	White	€16.95/12.95*	16
Petit Chardonnay 2018, Ken Forrester Wines	White	€14.95	27
Albarino 2017, Rias Baixas, Lagar de Costa	White	€19.95/ 16.95*	34
Julia Florista Branco, NV	White	€9.50/ 7.50*	25
Old Vine Reserve Chenin Blanc 2018, Ken Forrester	White	€17.95	46
Wildflower Pinot Noir 2018	Red	€13.95/8.35*	59
Le Temps des C(e)rises 2014, Santenay, Domaine Olivier	Red	€29.95/ 23.95*	86
Ars in Vitro 0216, Tandem, Valle de Yerri, Navarra	Red	€14.95	98
Petit Sao 2015, Costers del Segre	Red	€15.95	116
Reminat Primitivo 2018, IGT Terre di Chieti	Red	€18.95	120
D.O.C. Malbec 2016, Norton, Lujan de Cuyo,	Red	€18.95/ 12.95*	121
Dedicace 2017, Lirac, Domaine Coudoulis	Red	€19.95/ 26.95*	122
Vola Vole 2018, Trebbiano d'Abruzzo	White	€17.95/13.95*	134
Oloroso, Marqués de Poley , Toro Albala	Fortified	€19.95	159

O'Donovan's, Cork, Odonovansofflicence.com

	Style	Price	Wine No.
Ruinart R de Ruinart Champagne NV	Sparkling	€58.40	5
d'Arenberg Hermit Crab 2016, Mclaren Vale	White	€16.95	45
Taylor's Late-Bottled Vintage Port 2014	Fortified	€24	160

O'Driscolls Off Licence, Co. Kerry

	Style	Price	Wine No.
Mitchell & Son Claret 2015, Bordeaux Superieur	Red	€15	61
Chablis 1er cru Vauleront 2015,La Chablisienne	White	€40	141

J.J. O'Driscoll, Ballinlough, jjodriscoll.ie

	Style	Price	Wine No.
Framingham Pinot Noir 2016, Marlborough	Red	€27.99	84

STOCKISTS CONTINUED	Style	Price	Wine No.
O'Neills, D8			
Côtes du Rhône Saint-Esprit 2017, Delas	Red	€16.95	117
The Parting Glass, Enniskerry; McHughs, Dublin 5, mchughs.ie			
Garzon Tannat Reserva 2017,	Red	€20	124
PoppySeed, Clarinbridge, PoppySeed.ie			
Roka Furmint 2018, Kog, Stajerska	White	€19.50	19
Les Vignes d'Oc Rouge Grenache / Merlot 2018	Red	€12.99	95
Power & Co, Lucan, power-wine.com			
Gambellara Classico 2018, Cantina di Gambellara	White	€15.95	29
Amalaya Torrontés Riesling 2018, Calchaquí Valley	White	€17.99	31
Red Island Wine Co. Skerries			
Gambellara Classico 2018, Cantina di Gambellara	White	€15.95	29
Amalaya Torrontés Riesling 2018, Calchaquí Valley	White	€17.99	31
Leirana, Albariño, Forjas del Salnes 2018, Rías Baixas	White	€25	38
Rosso Piceno 2017, Saladini Pilastri	Red	€15.95	62
Domaine Lardy Moulin-à-Vent Vieilles Vignes 2016	Red	€22	73
Altos Las Hormigas Tinto 2017, Mendoza	Red	€17.99	100
Sherazadze Donnafugatta 2018, Nero d'Avola	Red	€23	103
Redmonds of Ranelagh, redmonds.ie			
Charles Heidsieck Brut Réserve Champagne	Sparkling	€70	8
Herdade de Grous Branco 2017, VR Alentejo	White	€18	32
Reto 2018, Manchuela, Bodegas Ponce	White	€21	36
Ahearne Rosine Hvar 2017	Rosé	€38.99	57
Camino Real 2017 Ribera Sacra, Guímaro	Red	€26	79
Folk Machine 'Parts & Labor' Red 2016, California	Red	€26	81
Ch. Bellevue-La-Forêt 2016, Fronton	Red	€16	99
Altos Las Hormigas Tinto 2017, Mendoza	Red	€17.99	100
Sherazadze Donnafugatta 2018, Nero d'Avola	Red	€23	103
Mimetic 2018, Gallinas de Piel, Calatayud	Red	€19.99	123
Rioja Reserva 2012, Senora de Remelluri, Remelluri	Red	€32	127

STOCKISTS CONTINUED	Style	Price	Wine No.
Seleccion de Bodega Malbec 2016, Dona Paula	Red	€35	128
Ink 2018, Judith Beck, Burgenland	Red	€17.95	133
Pheasant's Tears Saperavi 2018	Red	€23.95	135
Unlitro 2018, Ampelia IGT Costa Toscana	Red	€24.50	138
Chablis 1er cru Vauleront 2015,La Chablisienne	White	€40	141
Viña Tondonia 2005, Bodegas Lopez de Heredia, Rioja Reserva Blanco	White	€45	144
Pretty Pony 2013, Kanaan Winery, Ningxia	Red	€49.99	149
Sandhi Sanford & Benedict Chardonnay 2016	White	€50	150
Tolpuddle Vineyard Pinot Noir 2015, Tasmania	Red	€62.99	154
Callejuela Manzanilla Fina NV	Fortified	€18	158

Red Nose Wines, Clonmel, rednosewine.com

	Style	Price	Wine No.
Amalaya Torrontés Riesling 2018, Calchaquí Valley	White	€17.99	31
Bourgueil 2017 La Coudraye, Y. Amirault	Red	€24	75
Garzon Tannat Reserva 2017,	Red	€20	124

Riney's, Sneem

	Style	Price	Wine No.
Côtes du Rhône Saint-Esprit 2017, Delas	Red	€16.95	117
Searsons, Monkstown, searsons.com; Solto Escola 2016, Vinho Verde, Portugal	White	€13.95	11
St. Joseph 'Grand Duc du Montillet' 2017, Monteillet	White	€38.00	43
Zephyr 2017, Les Deux Cols, Cotes du Rhone	White	€22.95	49
Clos Saint Yves 2016 Savannières, Domaine des Baumard	White	€36.75	53
Domaine Lardy Moulin-à-Vent Vieilles Vignes 2016	Red	€22	73
Silice 2017, Ribera Sacra	Red	€26.95	82
Sherazadze Donnafugatta 2018, Nero d'Avola	Red	€23	103
Chemin des Fonts 2018, Les Deux Cols, C. du Rhône	Red	€28.50	111

Sheridan's Cheesemongers, Dublin 2, Kells, Co. Meath, Galway sheridanscheesemongers.com

	Style	Price	Wine No.
Arbois 'Cuvée d'Automne' Domaine de la Pinte 2016	White	€33.50	52
Marzemino 2018 Roberta Fugatti, IGT	Red	€16	64
Colle Morino 2017, Barba, Montepulciano d'Abruzzo	Red	€16.50	65

STOCKISTS CONTINUED	Style	Price	Wine No.
di Gino 2017, Rosso Piceno San Lorenzo	Red	€21.50	71
Bourgueil 2017 La Coudraye, Y. Amirault	Red	€24	75
Sancerre Rouge La Croix du Roy 2014, Lucien Crochet	Red	€34	88
Custoza Boscroi 2018, Monte dei Roari	White	€17	131
Bardolino "Reboi" 2018, Monte dei Roari	Red	€17	132
Verdicchio dei Castelli di Jesi 2018, San Michele	White	€24	137
Brunello di Montalcino 2014, Col d'Orcia	Red	€48	147

Shiel's, Malahide

	Style	Price	Wine No.
d'Arenberg Hermit Crab 2016, Mclaren Vale	White	€16.95	45
Passo Sardo 2016, Cannonau di Sardegna	Red	€14	115
Côtes du Rhône Saint-Esprit 2017, Delas	Red	€16.95	117

SIYPS.com

	Style	Price	Wine No.
Trenzado 2018, Suerte del Marqués, Tenerife	White	€26	23
Cucú 2018, Barco del Corneta, Rueda	White	€17.75	30
Reto 2018, Manchuela, Bodegas Ponce	White	€21	36
Terrasse 2017, Keermont, Stellenbosch	White	€30	50
Arbois 'Cuvée d'Automne' Domaine de la Pinte 2016	White	€33.50	52
Marzemino 2018 Roberta Fugatti, IGT	Red	€16	64
Colle Morino 2017, Barba, Montepulciano d'Abruzzo	Red	€16.50	65
di Gino 2017, Rosso Piceno San Lorenzo	Red	€21.50	71
Ch. Jean Faux Les Sources 2014, Bordeaux	Red	€26	80
Sancerre Rouge La Croix du Roy 2014, Lucien Crochet	Red	€34	88
Rouge-Gorge 2017, Coteaux de Loir Domaine de Bellivière	Red	€39	90
Chemin des Fonts 2018, Les Deux Cols, C. du Rhône	Red	€28.50	111
Custoza Boscroi 2018, Monte dei Roari	White	€17	131
Bardolino "Reboi" 2018, Monte dei Roari	Red	€17	132
Verdicchio dei Castelli di Jesi 2018, San Michele	White	€24	137
Brunello di Montalcino 2014, Col d'Orcia	Red	€48	147
2016 Chablis 1er Cru Mont de Milieu, Domaine Christophe	White	€49	148
Callejuela Manzanilla Fina NV	Fortified	€18	158

stationtostationwine.ie; wineonline.ie

	Style	Price	Wine No.
Gambellara Classico 2018, Cantina di Gambellara	White	€15.95	29

STOCKISTS CONTINUED	Style	Price	Wine No.
Viré-Clessé 2017, Les Pierres Blanches, André Bonhomme	White	€22.95	48
Ahearne Rosine Hvar 2017	Rosé	€38.99	57
Beaujolais '69' 2017, Christophe Coquard	Red	€16	63
Folk Machine 'Parts & Labor' Red 2016, California	Red	€26	81
Framingham Pinot Noir 2016, Marlborough	Red	€27.99	84
Altos Las Hormigas Tinto 2017, Mendoza	Red	€17.99	100
Viano 'Hillside" Red NV	Red	€18	101
Clos des Fous 'Pour ma Gueule" 2017, Itata Valley	Red	€19.99	102
Daniel Bouland Morgon Courcelette Vieilles Vignes 2016	Red	€26	109
Mimetic 2018, Gallinas de Piel, Calatayud	Red	€19.99	123
Sandhi Pinot Noir 2016, Sta. Rita Hills, California	Red	€38	140
Sandhi Sanford & Benedict Chardonnay 2016	White	€50	150
Trefiano 2015, Carmignano Riserva 2015, Cappezzana	Red	€54.99	152
Tolpuddle Vineyard Pinot Noir 2015, Tasmania	Red	€62.99	154

SuperValu, Supervalu.ie

	Style	Price	Wine No.
Santa Rita 120 Cabernet Franc	Red	€12.50	93
Carmen Gran Reserva Cabernet Sauvignon 2017	Red	€18.50	119

Swans on the Green, Naas

	Style	Price	Wine No.
Garzon Tannat Reserva 2017,	Red	€20	124
Chablis 1er cru Vauleront 2015,La Chablisienne	White	€40	141

Sweeney's D3, sweeneysd3.ie

	Style	Price	Wine No.
Soalheiro Alvarinho 2018, Vinho Verde	White	€21	21
Friulano 2018, Volpe Pasini, Friuli Colli Orientale	White	€15.50	28
Cucú 2018, Barco del Corneta, Rueda	White	€17.75	30
Clima 2016, Vale da Capucha IG Lisboa	White	€20	35
Passo Sardo 2016, Cannonau di Sardegna	Red	€14	115
Chablis 1er cru Vauleront 2015,La Chablisienne	White	€40	141
Viña Tondonia 2005, Bodegas Lopez de Heredia, Rioja Reserva Blanco	White	€45	144
As Sortes 2017, Rafael Palacios, Valdeorras	White	€46	146
Taylor's Late-Bottled Vintage Port 2014	Fortified	€24	160

Terroirs, Dublin 4, Terroirs.ie

	Style	Price	Wine No.
Le Vin est une Fête 2017, C. Marmandais, Elian da Ros	Red	€16.95	66

STOCKISTS CONTINUED	Style	Price	Wine No.
Chinon Vieilles Vignes 2017, Domaine Philippe Alliet	Red	€29.50	85
La Porte Saint Jean, Saumur 2015 , Sylvain Dittière	Red	€39.50	91
Iroulegy Tradition 2015, Domaine Arretxea	Red	€29.50	112
Pretty Pony 2013, Kanaan Winery, Ningxia	Red	€49.99	149
Trefiano 2015, Carmignano Riserva 2015, Cappezzana	Red	€54.99	152
Taylor's Late-Bottled Vintage Port 2014	Fortified	€24	160

Tesco, Tesco.ie

Tesco Finest Côtes de Gascogne 2018	White	€9	24
Santa Rita 120 Cabernet Franc	Red	€12.50	93

Thomas's of Foxrock

Charles Heidsieck Brut Réserve Champagne	Sparkling	€70	8
Domaine Lardy Moulin-à-Vent Vieilles Vignes 2016	Red	€22	73
Ch. Bellevue-La-Forêt 2016, Fronton	Red	€16	99
Chablis 1er cru Vauleront 2015,La Chablisienne	White	€40	141

Thomas Woodberrys, Galway, Woodberrys.ie

Terroir Unico Chardonnay 2018, Vina Zorzal	White	€18.50	33
Sherazadze Donnafugatta 2018, Nero d'Avola	Red	€23	103

The Vintry, Dublin 6 vintry.ie

Charles Heidsieck Brut Réserve Champagne	Sparkling	€70	8
Beaujolais '69' 2017, Christophe Coquard	Red	€16	63
Ch. Bellevue-La-Forêt 2016, Fronton	Red	€16	99
Altos Las Hormigas Tinto 2017, Mendoza	Red	€17.99	100
Chablis 1er cru Vauleront 2015,La Chablisienne	White	€40	141

The Vineyard, Galway

Ch. Bellevue-La-Forêt 2016, Fronton	Red	€16	99

Whelehans Wines, Co Dublin, whelehanswines.ie

Charles Heidsieck Brut Réserve Champagne	Sparkling	€70	8
Vermentino di Sardegna 2018, Sella & Mosca	White	€14.50	26
Herdade de Grous Branco 2017, VR Alentejo	White	€18	32
Leirana, Albariño, Forjas del Salnes 2018, Rías Baixas	White	€25	38
Kershaw Clonal Selection Chardonnay 2017	White	€54	54
La Roncière Pinot Noir 2017, Val de Loire, André Vatan	Red	€17	67
Bourgogne 2017, Domaine Derey Frères	Red	€24.50	10

	Style	Price	Wine No.
OCKISTS CONTINUED			
arzon Tannat Reserva 2017,	Red	€20	124
ateau Beauchene Premier Terroir 2016,			
tes du Rhone	Red	€20	125
oja Reserva 2012, Senora de Remelluri, Remelluri	Red	€32	127
ia Tondonia 2005, Bodegas Lopez de Heredia,			
oja Reserva Blanco	White	€45	144
villon de Léoville Poyferré 2015, St. Julien	Red	€45	145
Sortes 2017, Rafael Palacios, Valdeorras	White	€46	146
llejuela Manzanilla Fina NV	Fortified	€18	158

e Wine Centre, Kilkenny, Thewinecentre.ie

	Style	Price	Wine No.
oja Reserva 2012, Senora de melluri, Remelluri	Red	€32	127

hite Gables, Moycullen, Co. Galway, whitegables.com

	Style	Price	Wine No.
sso Piceno 2017, Saladini Pilastri	Red	€15.95	62

e Wine House, Trim

	Style	Price	Wine No.
ima 2016, Vale da Capucha IG Lisboa	White	€20	35
Arenberg Hermit Crab 2016, Mclaren Vale	White	€16.95	45
tes du Rhône Saint-Esprit 2017, Delas	Red	€16.95	117
arzon Tannat Reserva 2017,	Red	€20	124
etty Pony 2013, Kanaan Winery, Ningxia	Red	€49.99	149
o Paddocks 'The Fusilier' Pinot Noir 2018,	Red	€50	151

ines Direct, Mullingar, and Arnotts, Dublin, winesdirect.ie

	Style	Price	Wine No.
hbilk Marsanne 2018, Nagambie Lakes	White	€14.25	13
uscadet de Sèvre & Maine, La Louvetrie	White	€17.15	17
not Noir, Domaine de la Renne, Val de Loire	Red	€14.15	60

ines on the Green, Dublin 2, Celticwhiskeyshop.com

	Style	Price	Wine No.
ollinger Special Cuvée Champagne NV	Sparkling	€55.65	4
inart R de Ruinart Champagne NV	Sparkling	€58.40	5
uros Antigos Vinho Verde 2018	White	€14	12
iulano 2018, Volpe Pasini, Friuli Colli Orientale	White	€15.50	28
n Year Old Malvasia, Barbeito, Madeira, NV	Fortified	€ 39.99	162

e Wicklow Wine Co., Wicklow, wicklowwineco.ie

	Style	Price	Wine No.
eto 2018, Manchuela, Bodegas Ponce	White	€21	36
llejuela Manzanilla Fina NV	Fortified	€18	158

ilde & Green, Dublin 6, wildeandgreen.com

	Style	Price	Wine No.
itchell & Son Claret 2015, Bordeaux Superieur	Red	€15	61
eurie Tradition 2016, Domaine de la Madone	Red	€20.95	70

	Style	Price	Wine No.
Wineonline.ie			
Bollinger Special Cuvée Champagne NV	Sparkling	€55.65	4
Gambellara Classico 2018, Cantina di Gambellara	White	€15.95	29
Amalaya Torrontés Riesling 2018, Calchaquí Valley	White	€17.99	31
Framingham Pinot Noir 2016, Marlborough	Red	€27.99	84
Clos des Fous 'Pour ma Gueule" 2017, Itata Valley	Red	€19.99	102
Imaginador 2017, Pedro Parra, Itata	Red	€26.99	110
Bodega Colomé 'Auténtico' Salta Malbec 2017	Red	€41.99	142
Pretty Pony 2013, Kanaan Winery, Ningxia	Red	€49.99	149
Taylor's Late-Bottled Vintage Port 2014	Fortified	€24	160
Worldwide Wines, Waterford, worldwidewines.ie			
Ruinart R de Ruinart Champagne NV	Sparkling	€58.40	5
Charles Heidsieck Brut Réserve Champagne	Sparkling	€70	8
Ch.du Coing de St. Fiacre 2017, Muscadet	White	€16.55	15
Terlaner Cuvée 2018, Trentino	White	€24.75	37
Masetto Nero 2016, Endrizzi, Vigneti delle Dolomiti	Red	€24.95	76
Cielo Rosso 2018 IGP Terre Siciliane	Red	€12.95	94
Benje Tinto, Envínate, 2017	Red	€28.00	139
Gabriela Pago Balbaina, Manzanilla	Fortified	€12.30*	157

*per 1/2 bottle

Notes